COLOR &
WRITE
HALLOWEEN
HAPPY HALLOWEEN
RIP
AF260838

Welcome to Color & Write!

Thank you for joining the adventure.

We created this book to spark creativity, imagination, and joyful learning. Color & Write is more than just a coloring book—it invites children to express themselves through imagination, writing and storytelling while exploring their artistic side.

Each design includes space to write, along with fun facts and playful prompts to help parents and caregivers guide younger children, while older children read and respond independently. Children can write Halloween facts and stories—or simply practice letters and words. Some may use the space to create their own art—or add to the design itself.

Some children will be drawn in by the artwork. Others may come for the writing and discover the joy of coloring. Either way, they're building skills on both sides of the brain—language and art working together.

With a wide range of designs, this book grows with your child—and can easily be shared among siblings and friends.

Be sure to check out the bonus section at the end: "Why Handwriting and Art Matter". You'll also find matching lined paper to duplicate for children who want to write more.

We hope Color & Write becomes a favorite in your home or classroom.

Warm wishes,
The Glenwood Treehouse

About Us: We are educators with decades of experience in K–12 classrooms and teacher preparation. This book blends what we know about how kids learn best—with creativity, joy, and room to grow. Look for our other Color & Write books!

Copyright © 2025 by The Glenwood Treehouse
All rights reserved. No portion of this book may be reproduced, distributed or transmitted in any form without written permission from the publisher or author, except as permitted by U.S. copyright law.

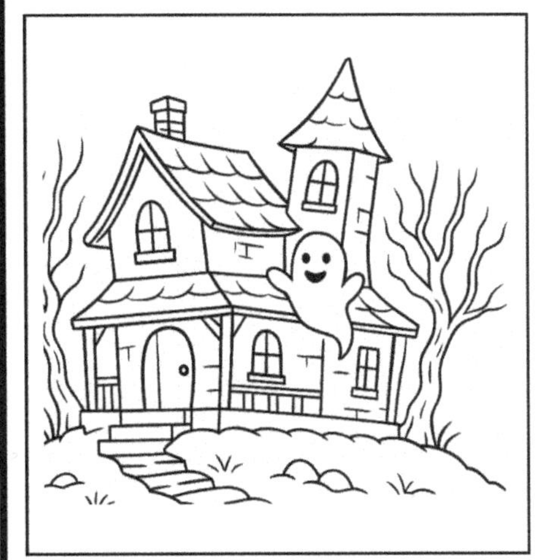 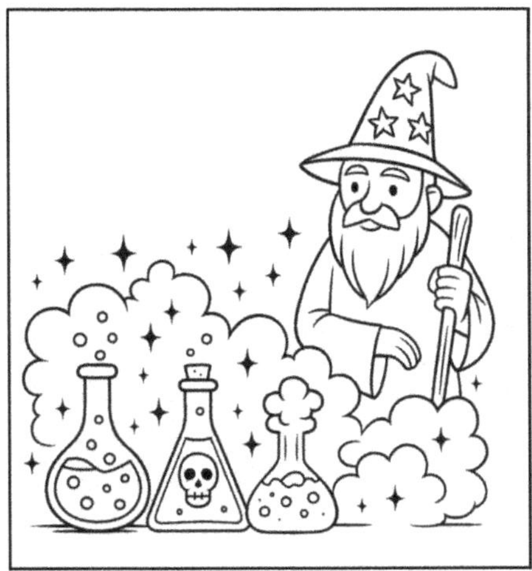 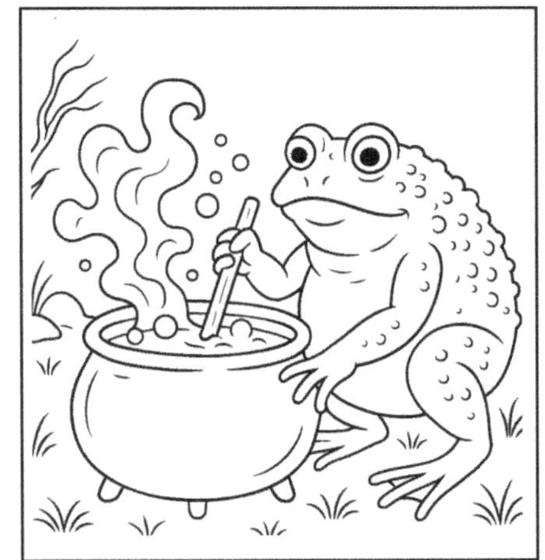

This Book Belongs To

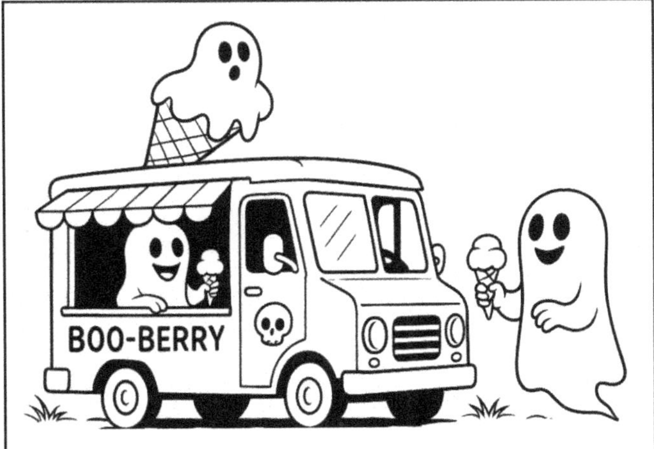

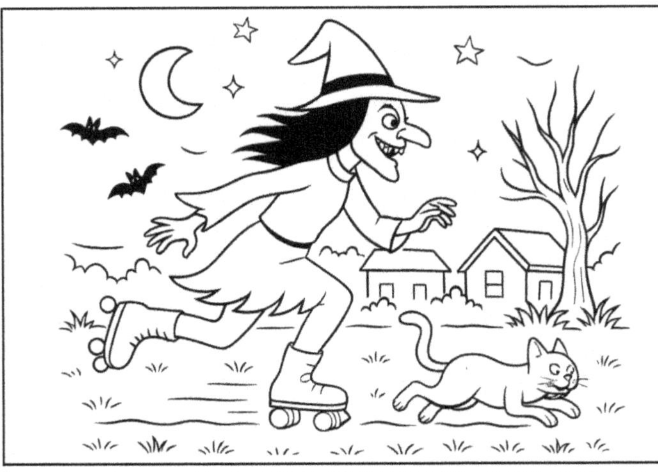

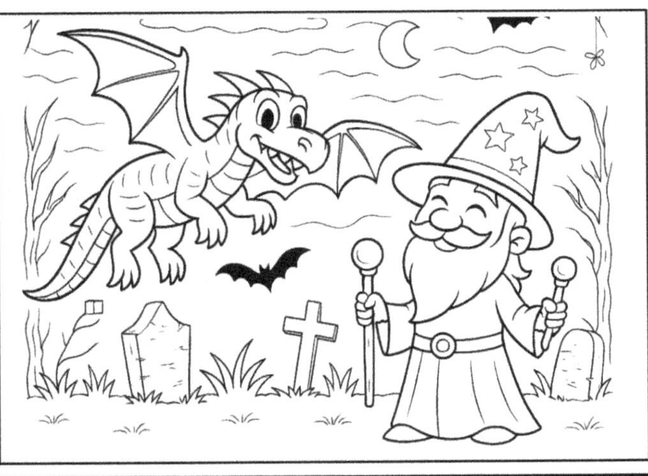

Happy Halloween

Halloween comes from a festival celebrated over 2000 years ago in Ireland and other Celtic nations. Irish and Scottish immigrants brought Halloween to the United States in the 1800's.

- What is your favorite thing to do on Halloween?
- If you were an immigrant, what tradition would you bring to your new country?

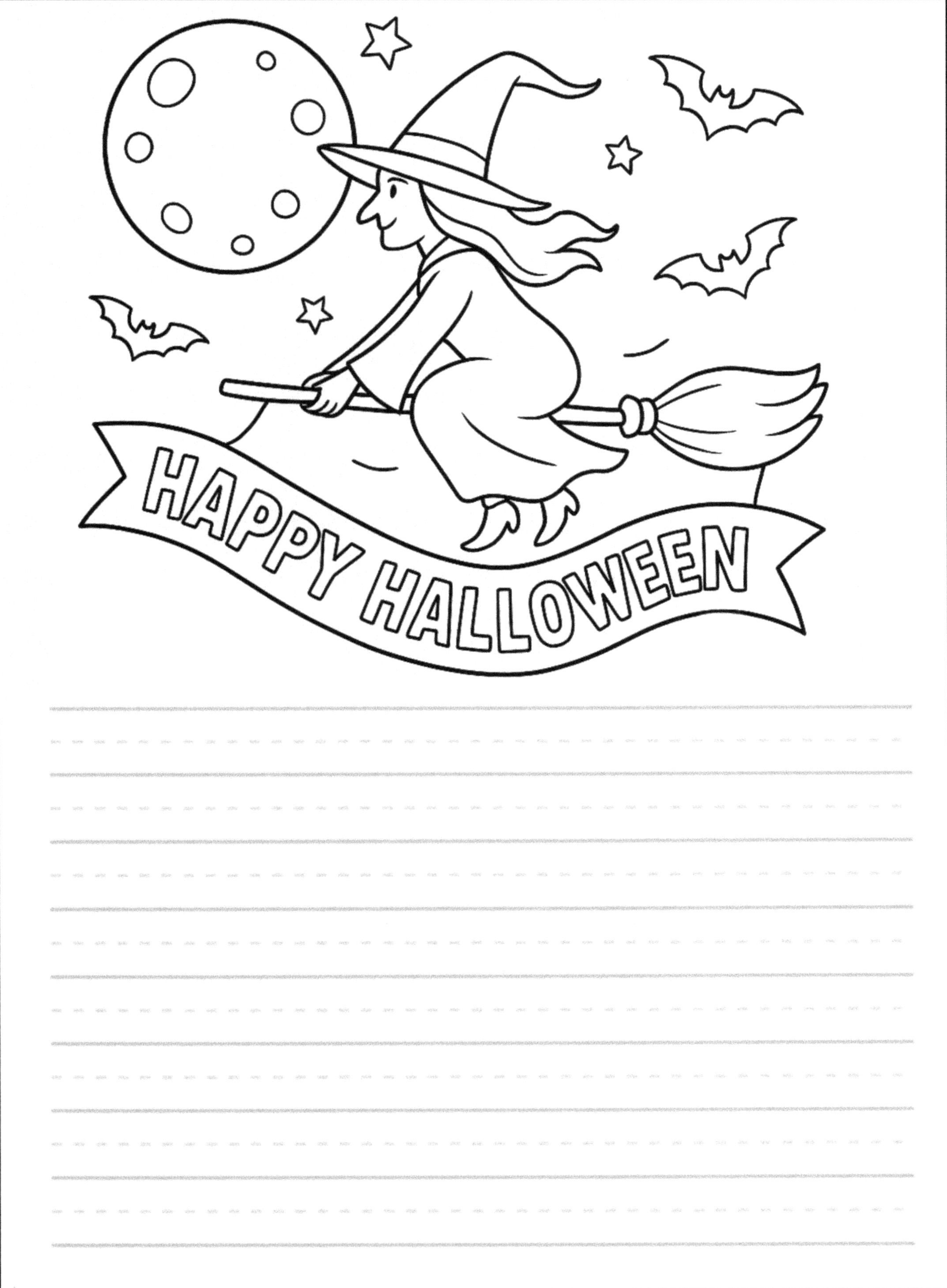

HAPPY HALLOWEEN

Haunted House

Old, empty houses can seem spooky, and some people think they might be haunted. But haunted houses at amusement parks are made for fun—you can feel scared and safe at the same time.

- If you were designing a haunted house, how would you make it scary but still safe?
- What sound effects would make a haunted house extra spooky?

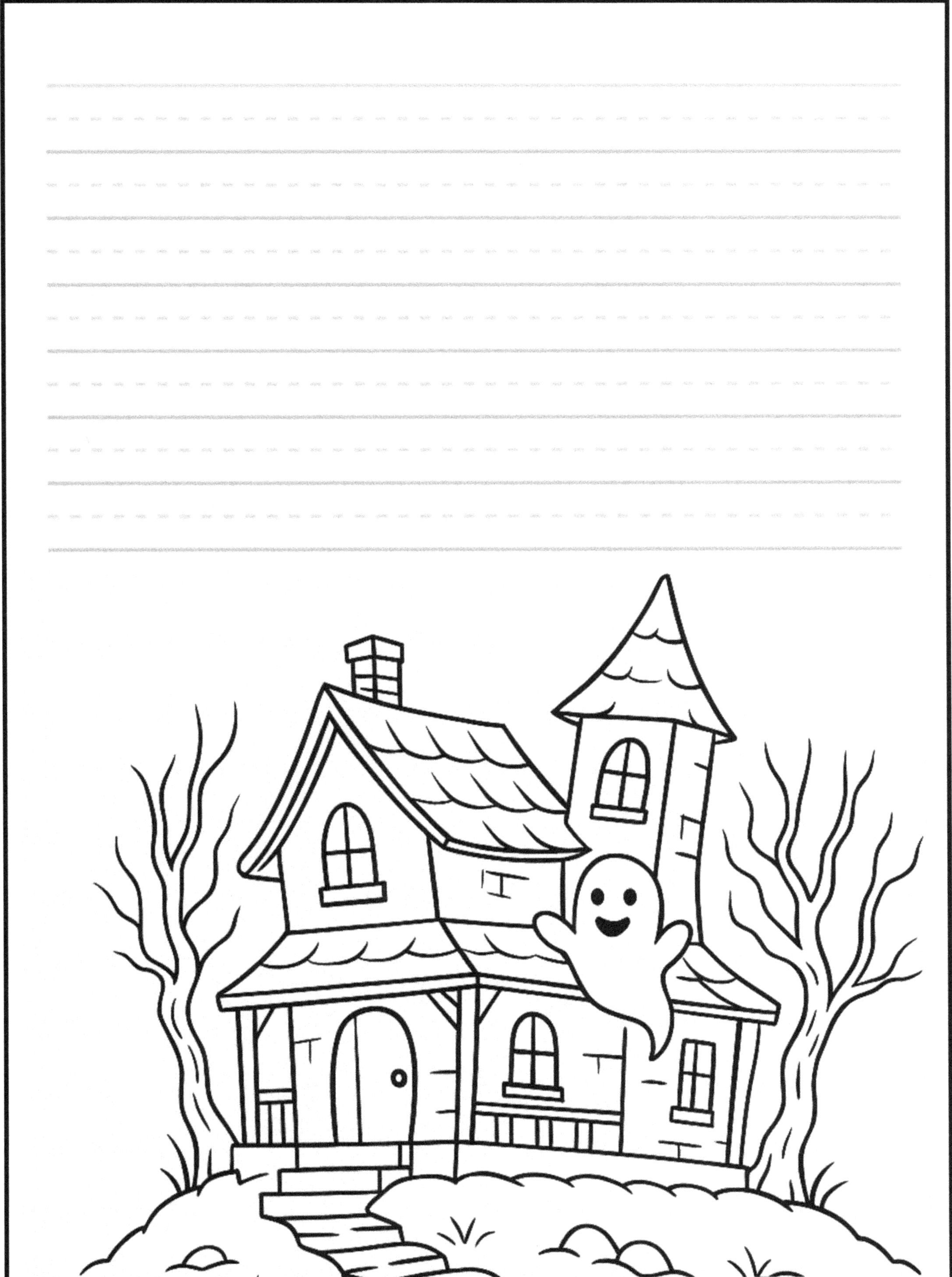

Pumpkins

The idea of carving pumpkins started with Irish immigrants who carved turnips to ward off evil spirits. In the United States, people began to carve pumpkins because they are easy to grow and to carve.

- Do you like funny pumpkins or scary pumpkins?
- Imagine a pumpkin that comes to life—what adventures would it have?

What Do Ghosts Say?

Most people imagine ghosts sneaking up and yelling "Boo!" But in other parts of the world, ghosts might giggle, whisper secrets, or sing a spooky tune instead. Ghosts can be surprising in lots of ways!

- What sound do you think a ghost would make?
- Write a story about a ghost who tries to scare kids, but the kids just laugh instead.

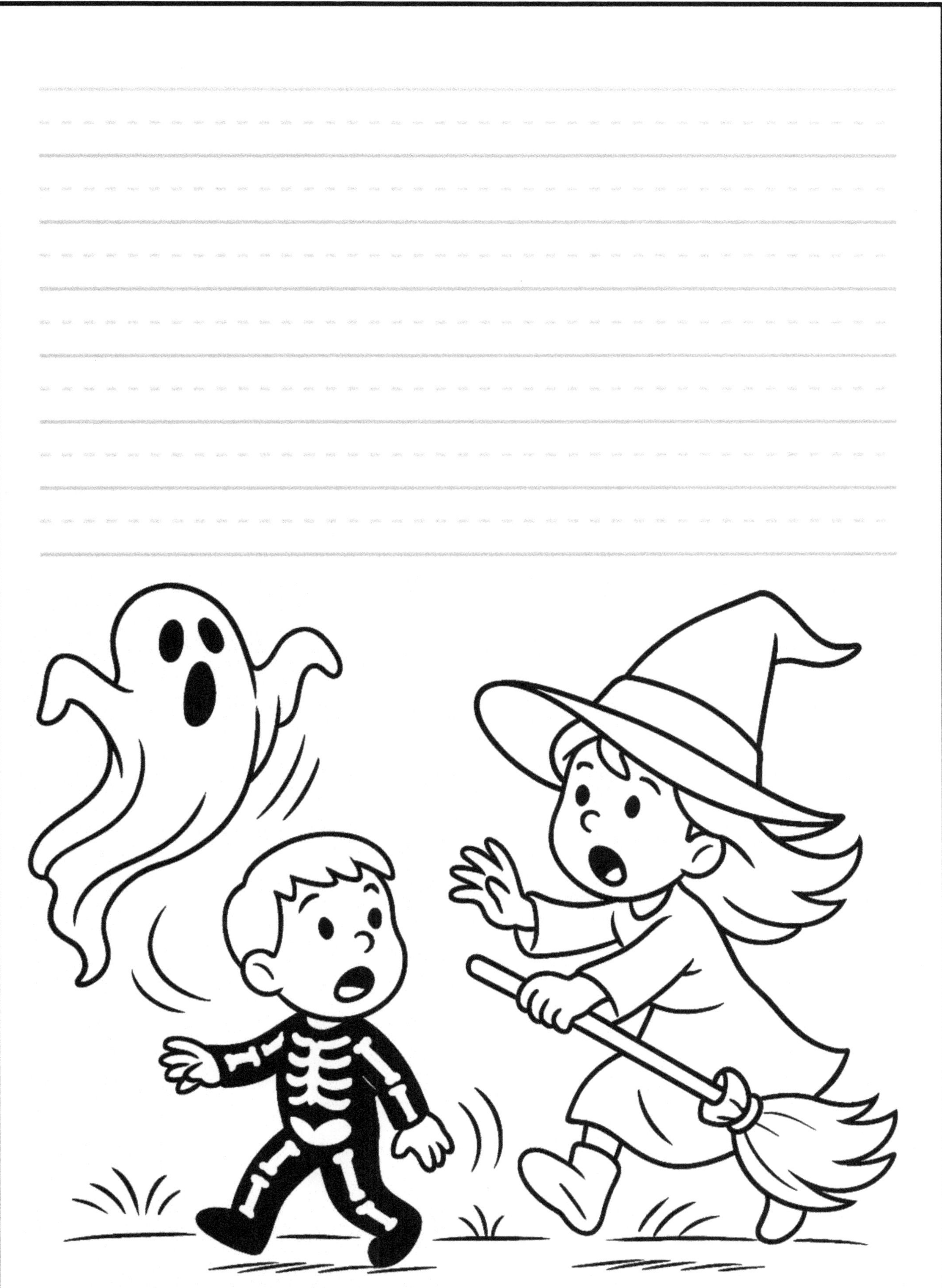

Wizard & Dragon

Dragons are make-believe creatures that show up in myths, legends, and even modern stories like Harry Potter. Sometimes wizards and dragons are friends, but dragons are often too powerful (and fiery!) to be pets.

- Can you make up a story about a wizard or a dragon?
- If you had your own dragon, what would you want it to do?

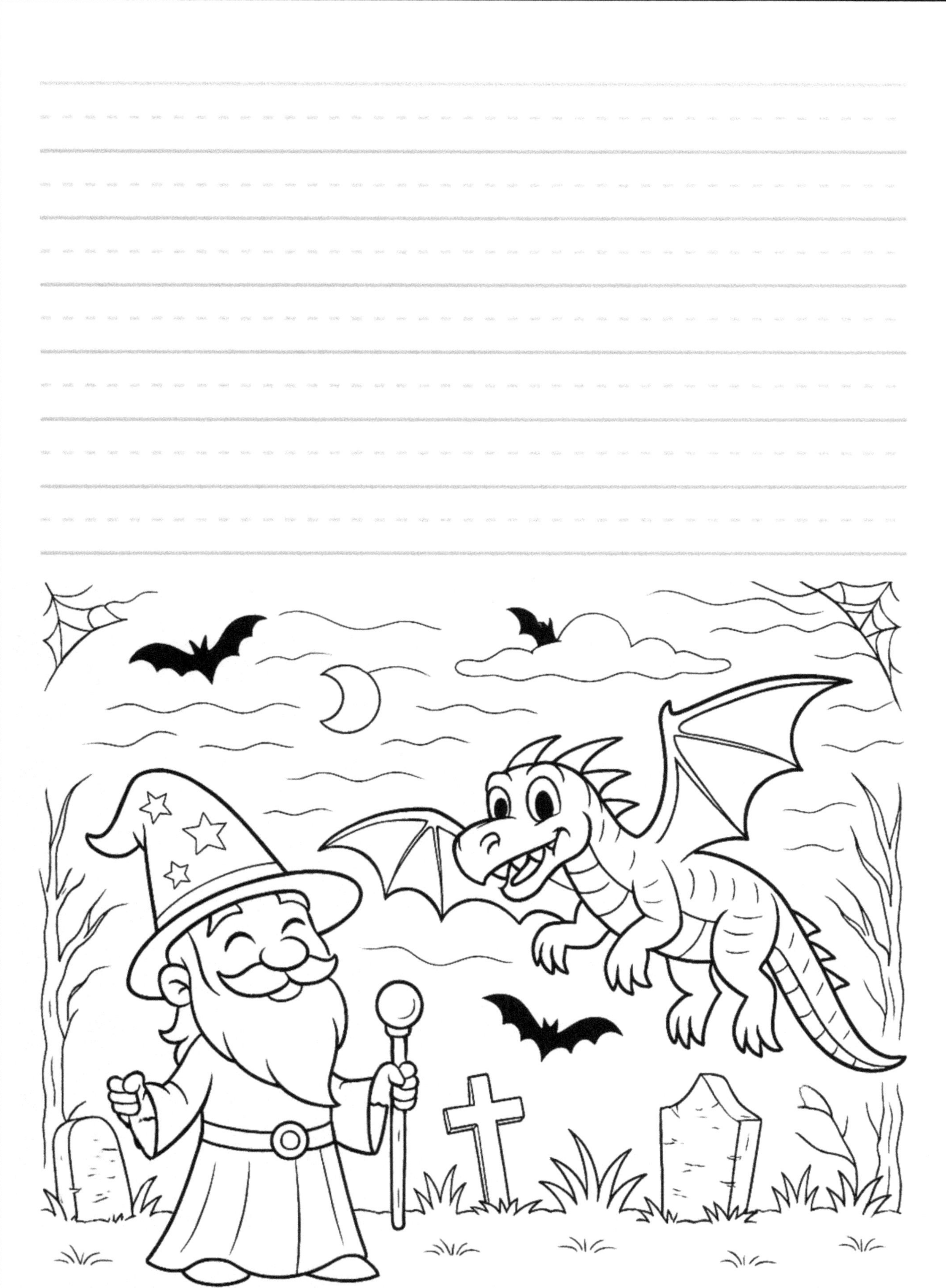

Funny Monsters

Not all monsters are scary. In some stories and movies, monsters are funny or helpful.

- Imagine your own silly or spooky monster. What makes it special?
- How would you calm a monster who is afraid of the dark?

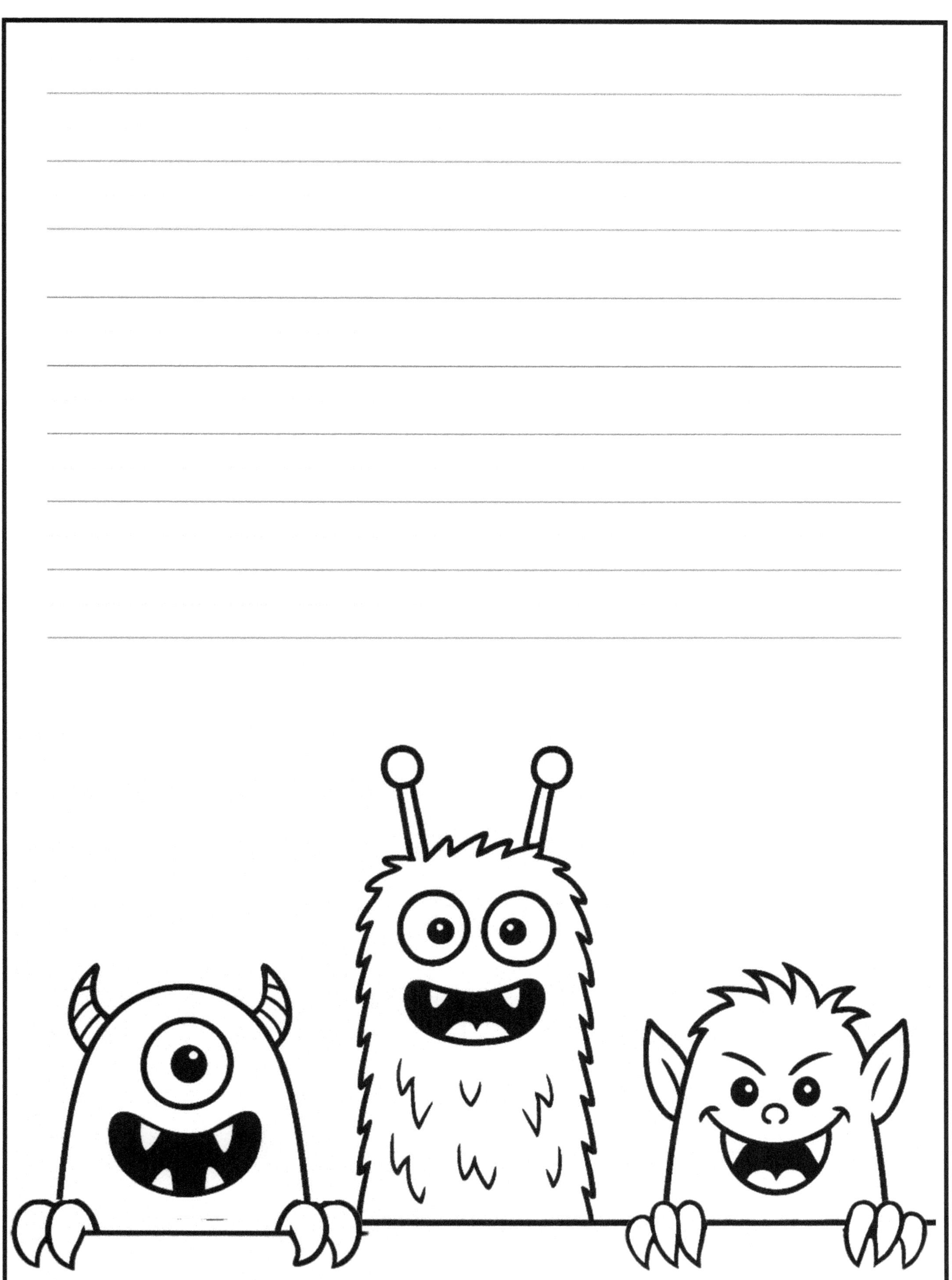

Zombies

In stories and movies, zombies are creatures who have come back to life. They are slow, stiff, and clumsy, and often don't seem to know where they are going.

- Do you think zombies are dangerous—or just confused?
- What would you do if a group of zombies showed up at your Halloween party?

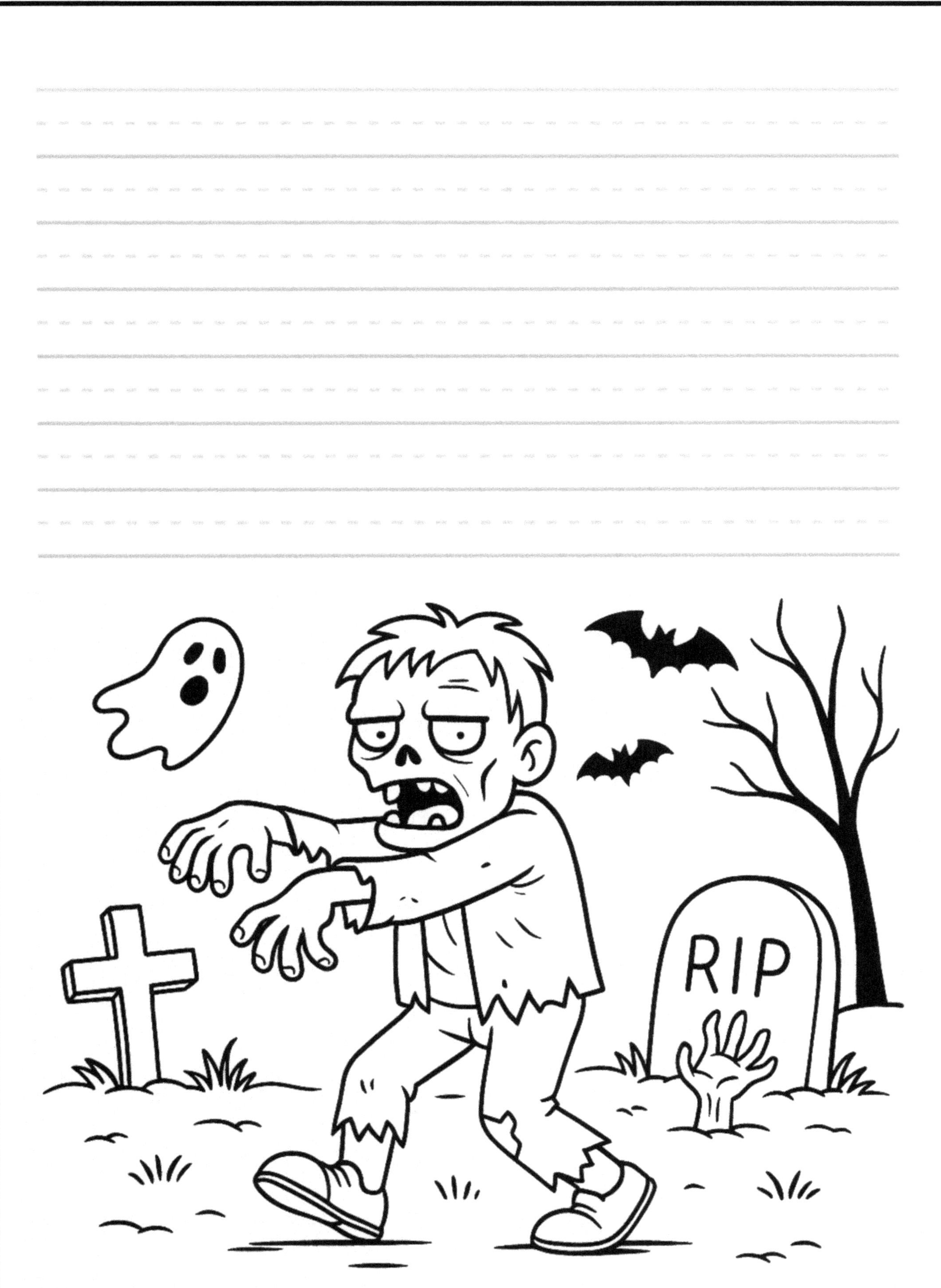

Witches

Witches have been part of folklore for hundreds of years. In fairy tales and fantasy, some witches are good, some are bad—and some are funny!

- Can you think of a witch from a story or movie? Was the witch good, evil, or silly?
- Would you want a witch as a friend? Why or why not?

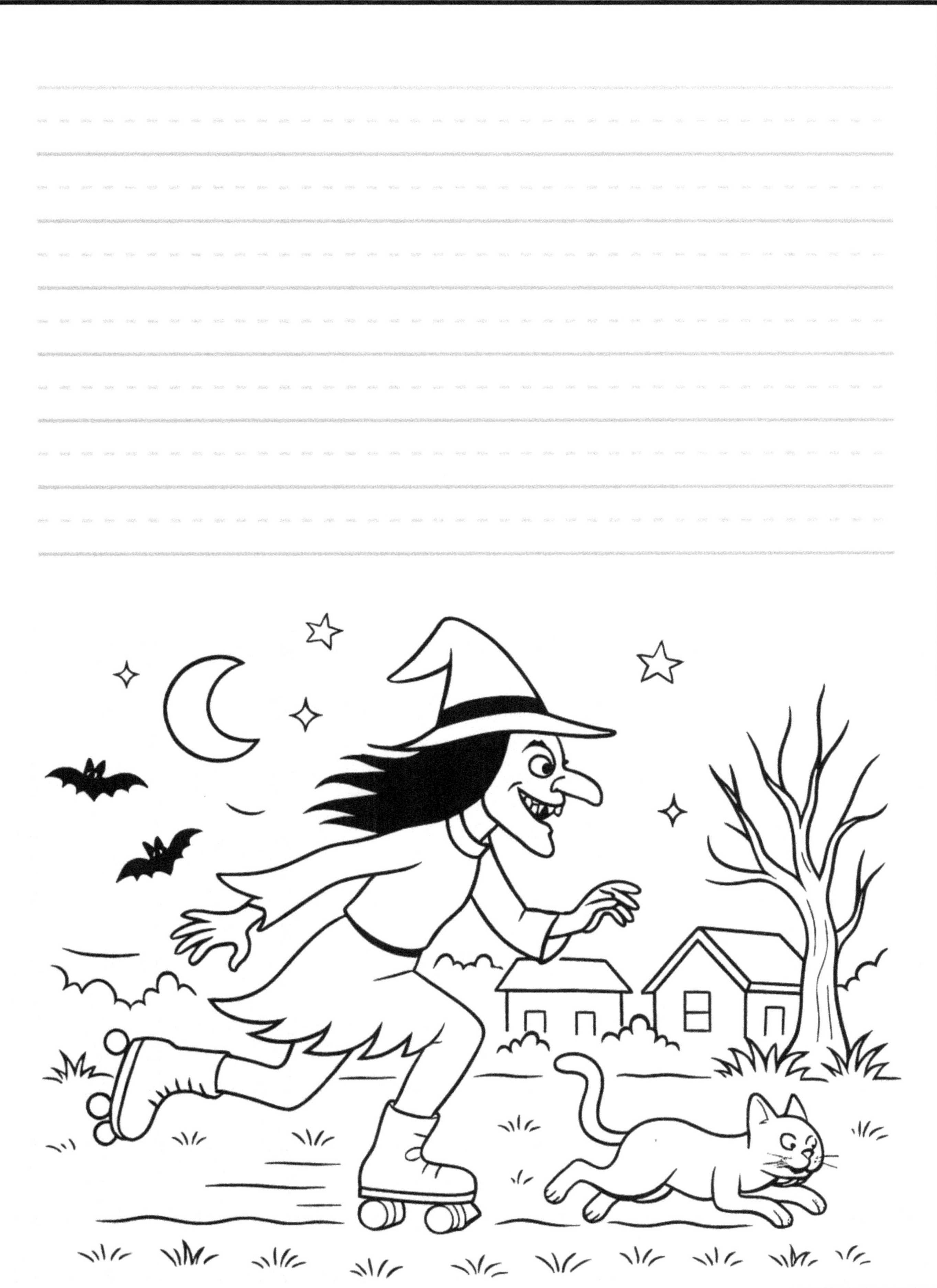

Frog

Warty frogs often appear in witch stories, sitting by the cauldron or hopping around while potions bubble. But sometimes, unlucky frogs get tossed right into the potion!

- Do you think frogs like hanging out with witches?
- If a witch's frog could talk, what spooky secrets might it tell?

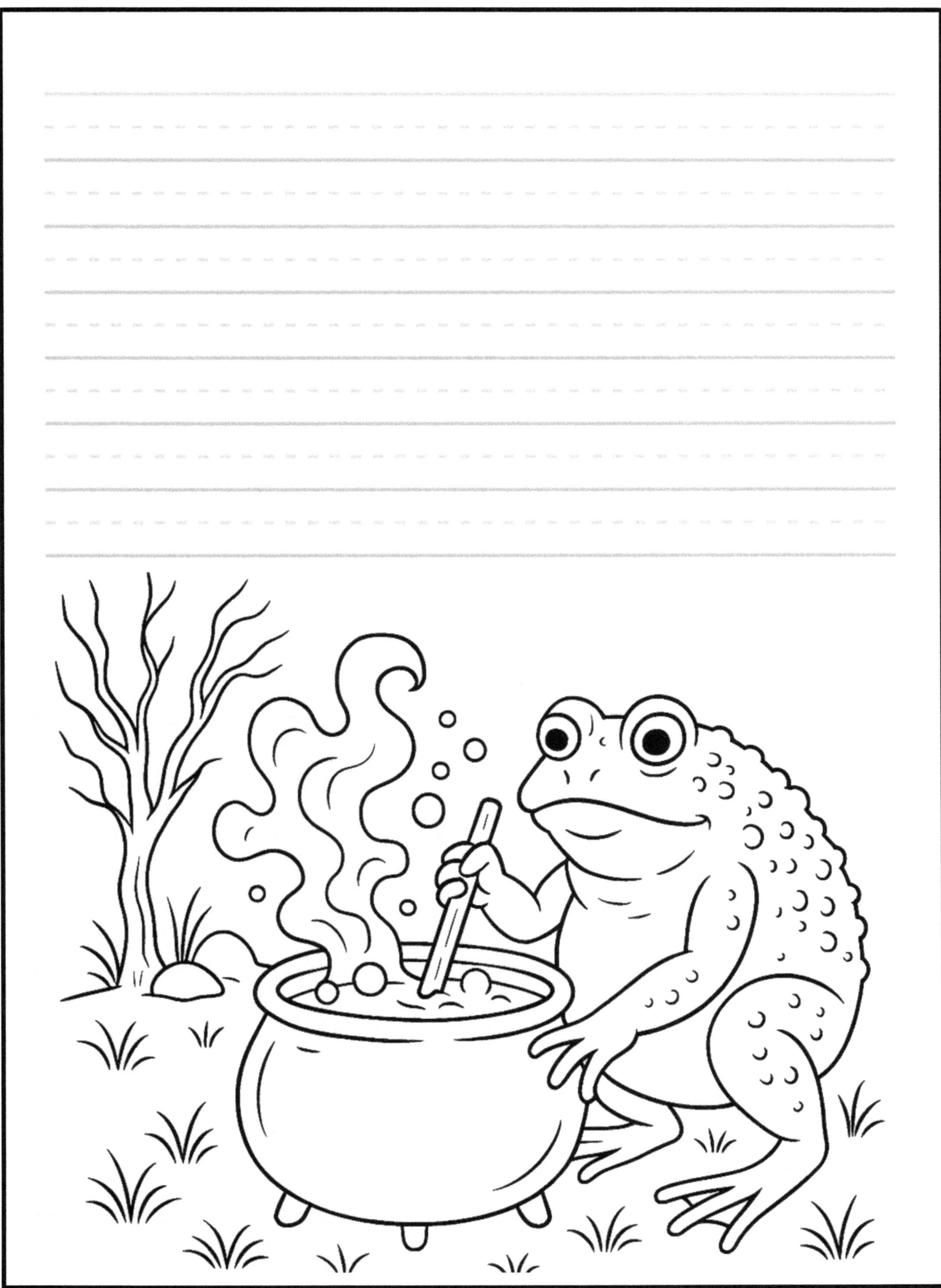

Ghost Ice Cream

If ghosts sold ice cream, their trucks might look spooky and cool—serving flavors like "Boo-Berry" or "Phantom Fudge."

- What other spooky ice cream flavors can you dream up? Give them funny names!
- Would you buy your treats from a ghost's ice cream truck?

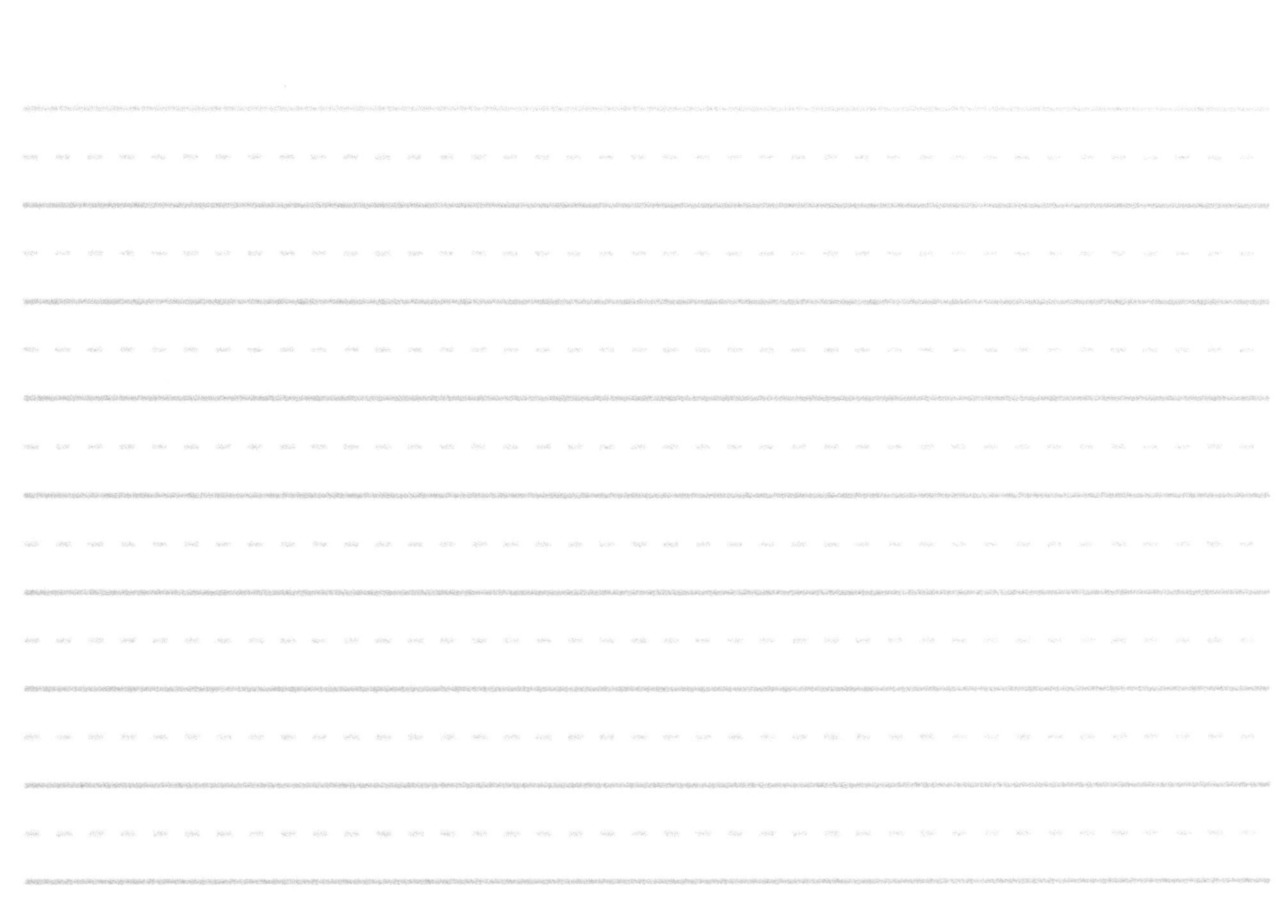

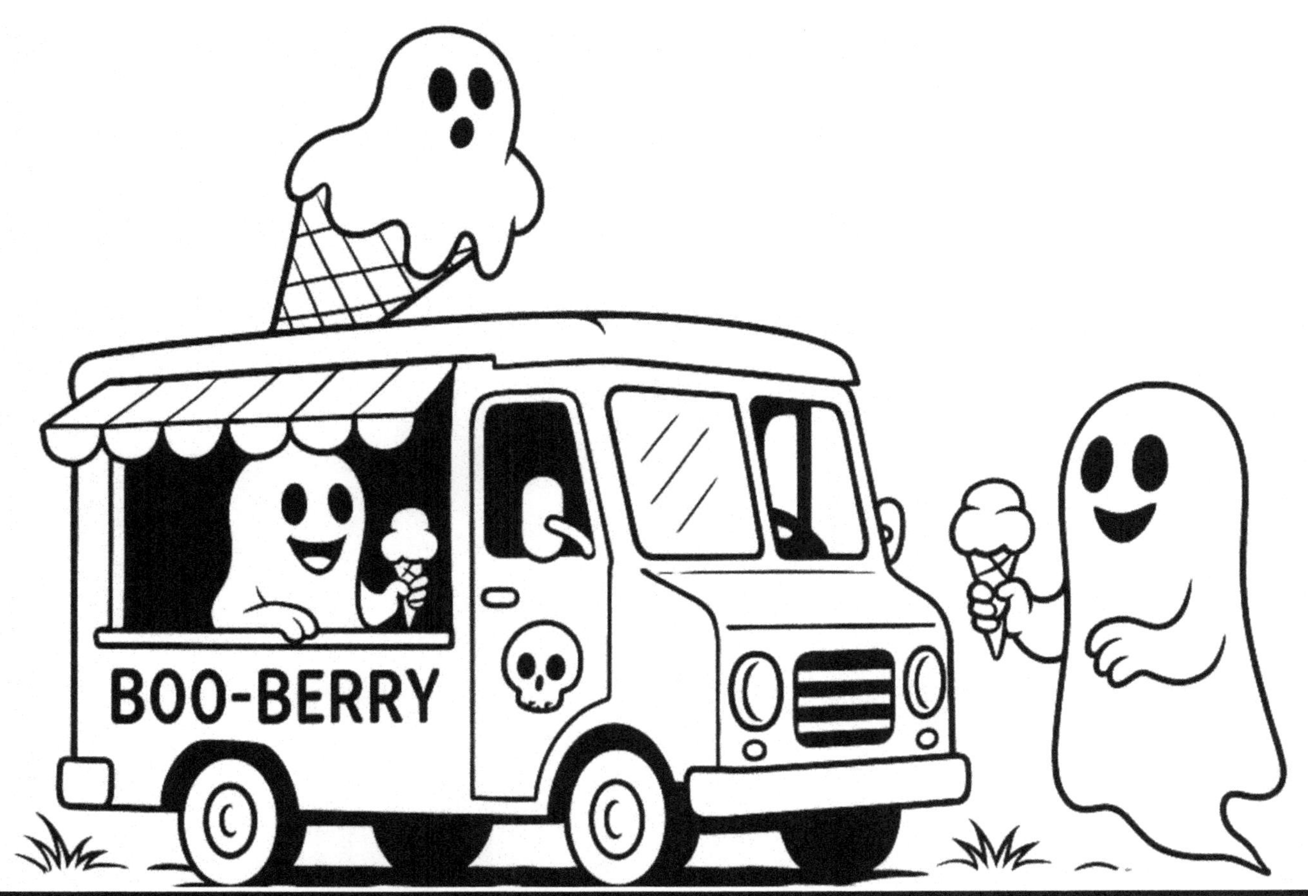
BOO-BERRY

Pets in Costume

Millions of people in the U.S. dress up their pets for Halloween. Some popular pet costumes are pumpkins, skeletons, hot dogs, and superheroes.

- If your pet or a pet you know could pick their own costume, what would it be?
- Do you think pets like getting dressed up—or not so much?

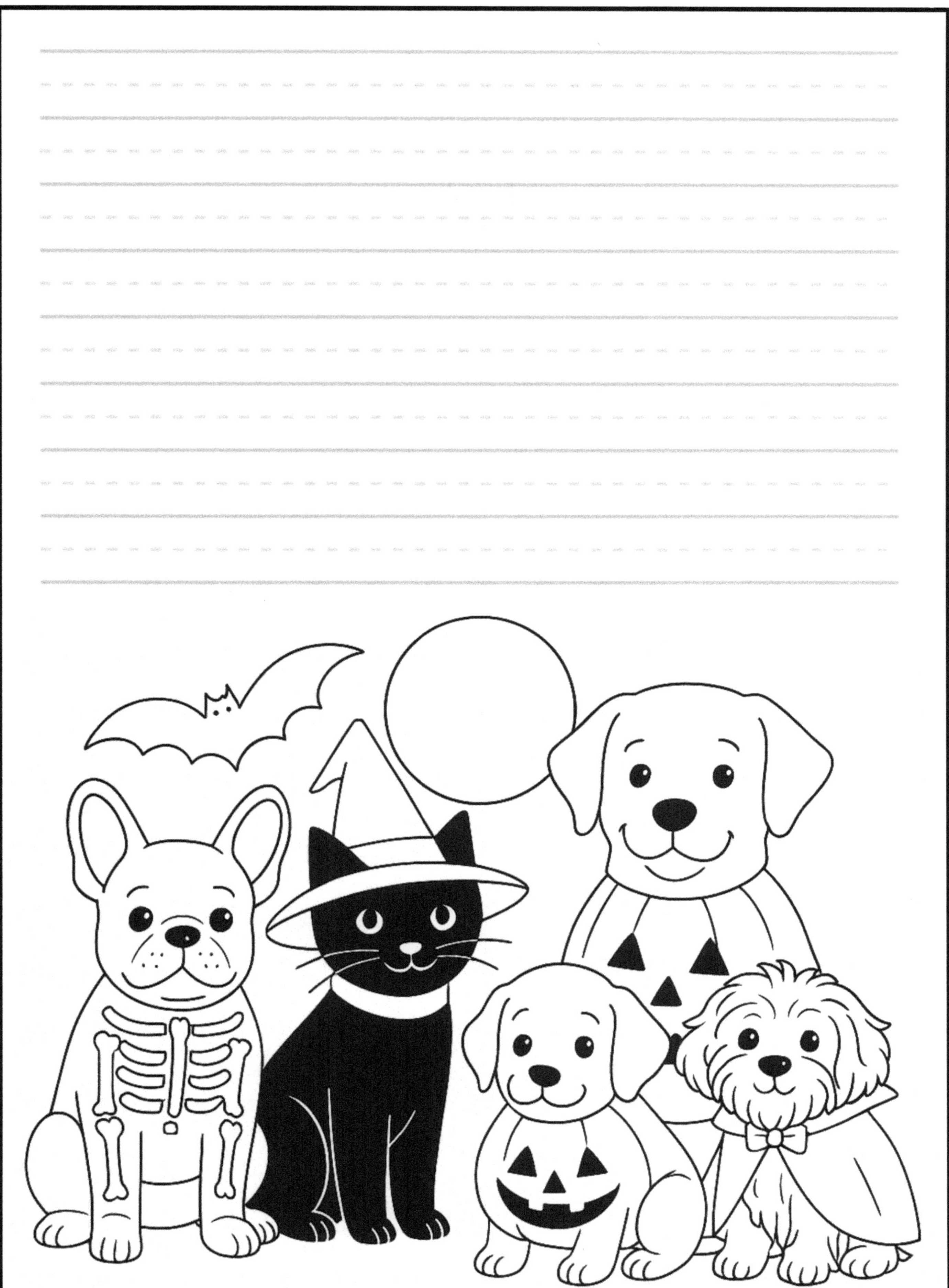

Witch & Wizard School

In many stories, young witches and wizards go to special schools to learn magic. Their classes might include things like "Flying 101", "Potion Mixing", or even "Care of Magical Creatures".

- What would you want to learn at a witch or wizard school?
- What do you think these witch and wizard kids are putting in their bubbling brew?

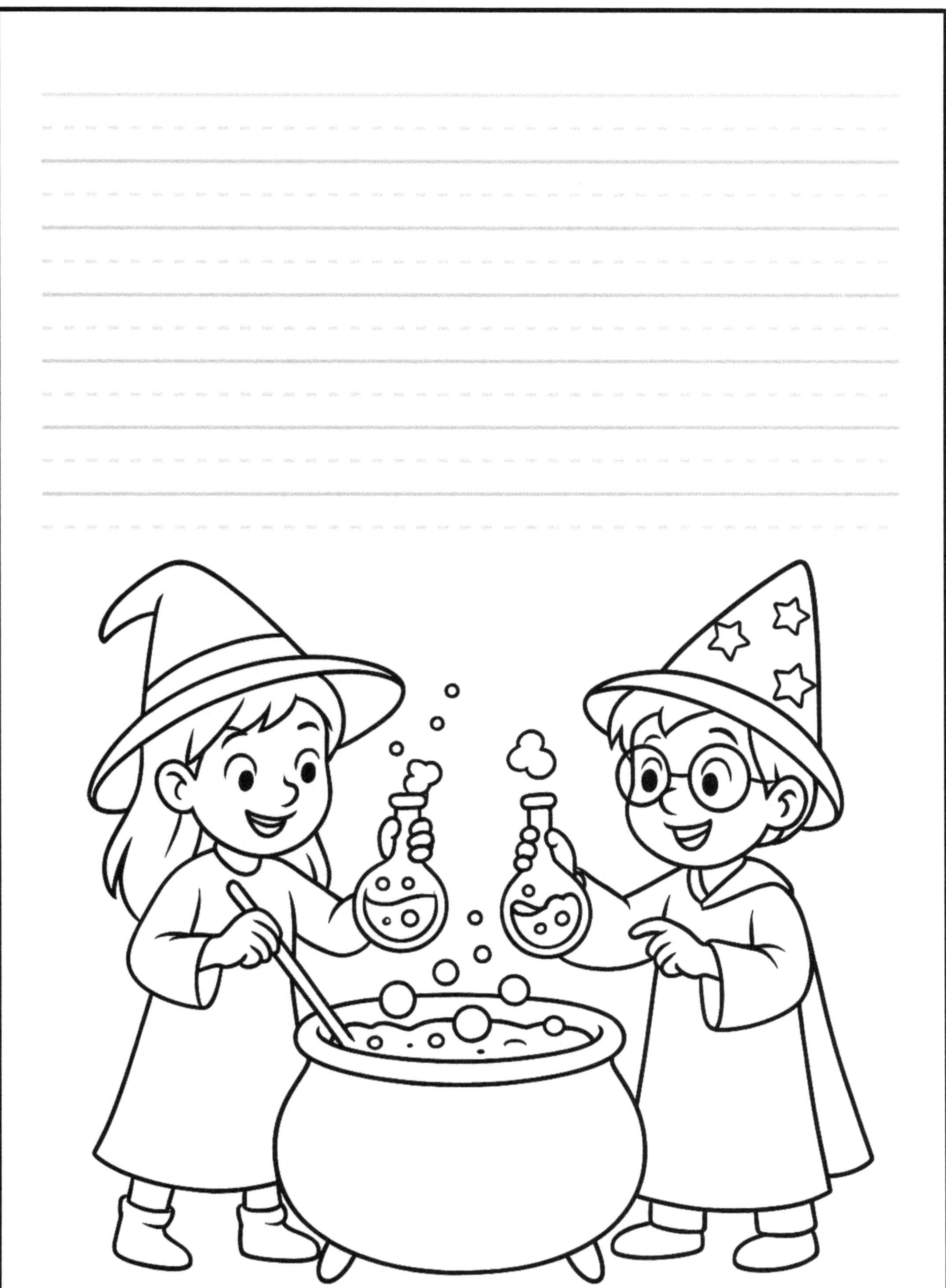

Cheerful Monsters

Not all monsters are scary. In many cartoons and movies, monsters are silly, kind, or even goofy. Bright colors, silly shapes, and funny features—like five eyes or polka-dotted fur—make them more fun than scary.

- What would a cheerful monster do on Halloween night?
- Create your own cheerful monster. What does it love to do? Use the space to draw it or write about it.

Skeleton Picnic

Skeletons may look spooky in the dark, but on Halloween they can be silly too—sometimes even sharing snacks at a picnic. That's part of the fun of Halloween—you never know what surprises you'll see!

- What would you do if some friendly Halloween skeletons showed up at your picnic?
- Imagine a funny skeleton. What kind of jokes do you think it would tell?

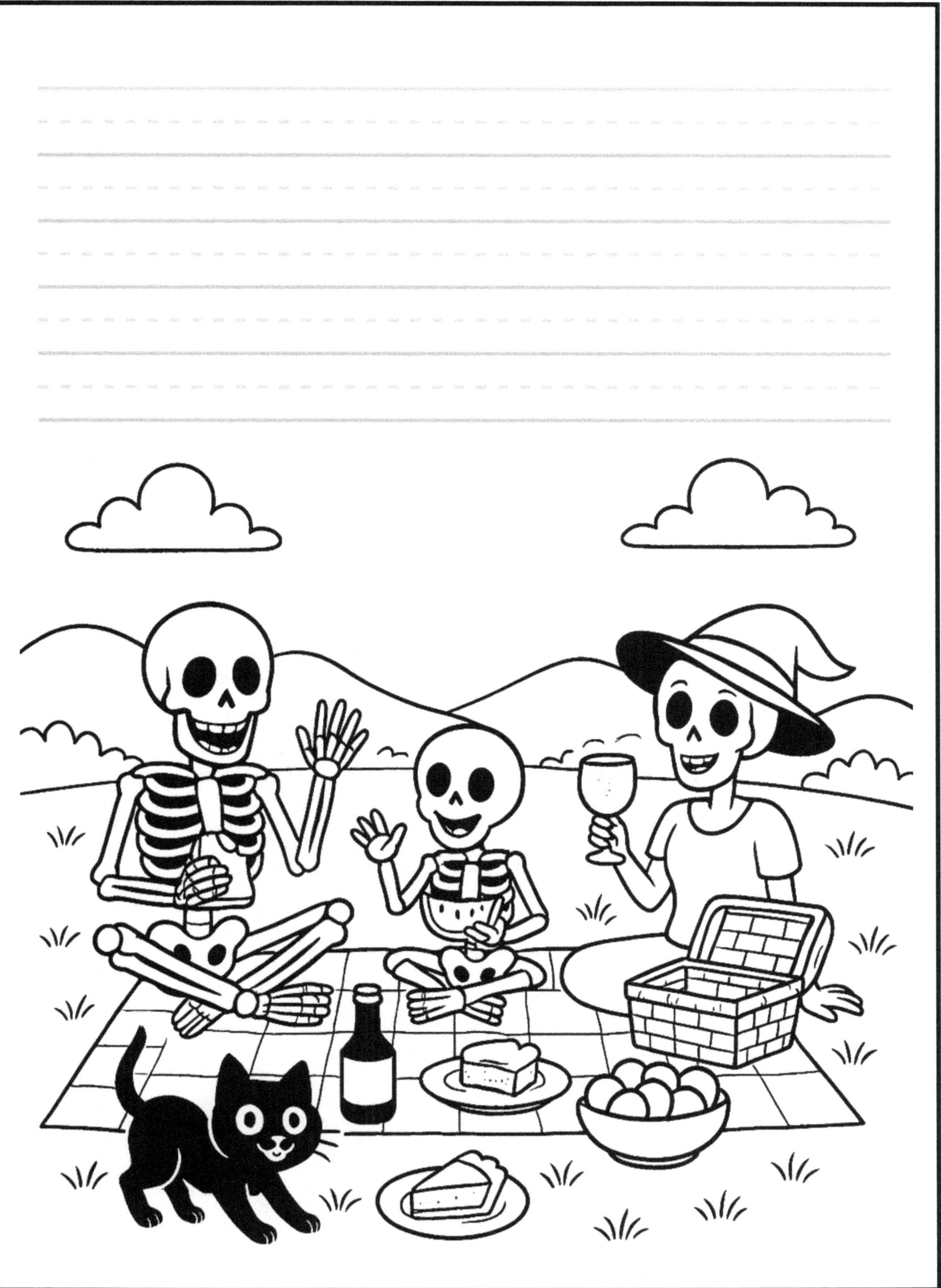

Witch's Laundry

Long ago, people believed that clotheslines could hold special energy. Some stories even say witches would hang magical items on a line to soak up moonlight or firelight.

- What do you think will happen to the items this witch is hanging on her clothes line?
- Tell a story about a kid who finds a piece of laundry with strange powers.

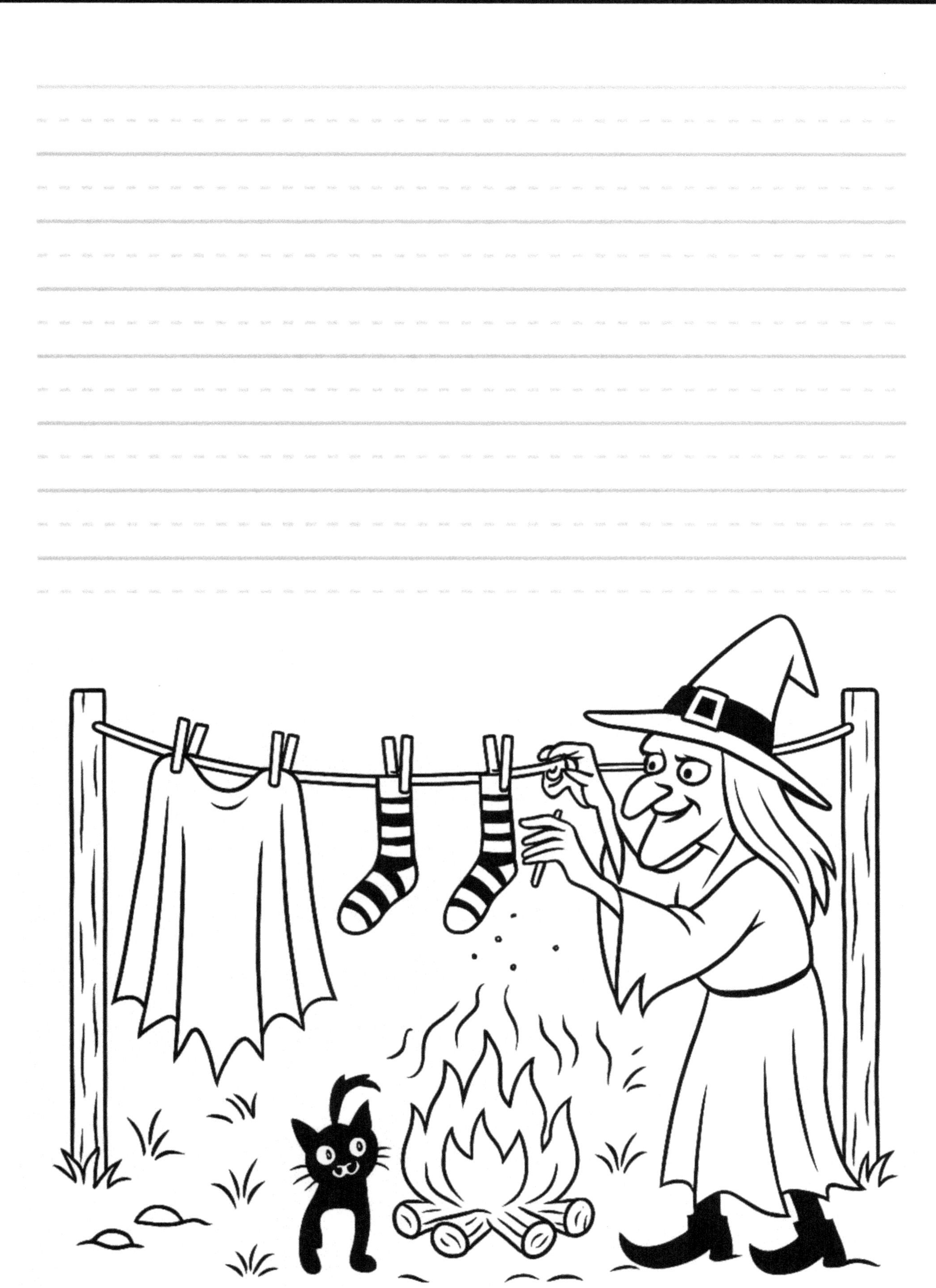

Halloween Border

Halloween decorations often mix many different fun and spooky items—like pumpkins, bats, ghosts, and more! Borders are a fun way to show many different Halloween symbols all together.

- How many different kinds of things can you find in this border?
- What's your favorite Halloween decoration? Is it spooky or funny?

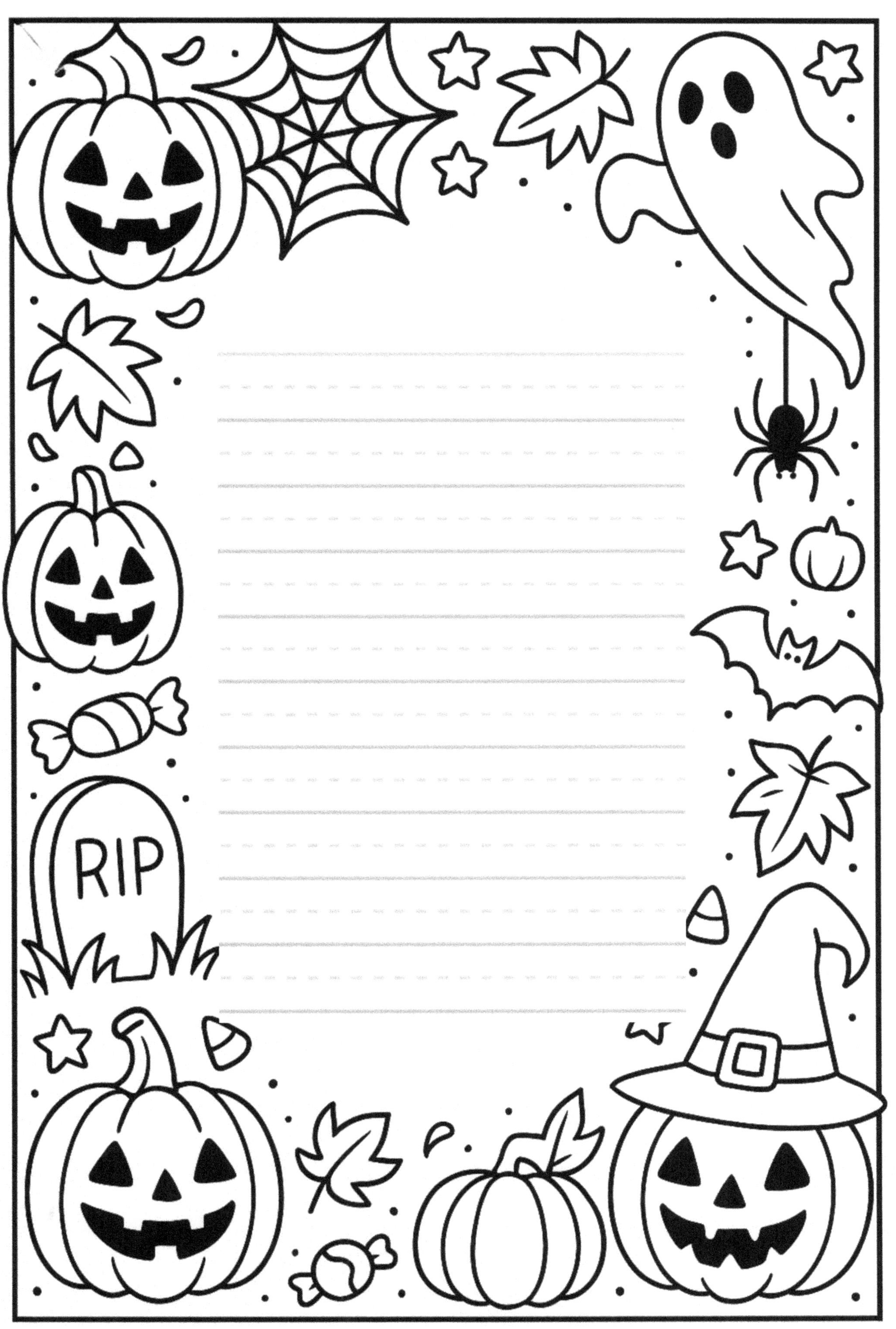

Spooky Mansion

When people see an old, broken-down mansion, they sometimes imagine it might be haunted. With creaky doors, cobwebs, and dark windows, it's easy to picture ghosts inside!

- What makes this mansion look spooky?
- What would you do if you were walking through the woods and saw a mansion like this?

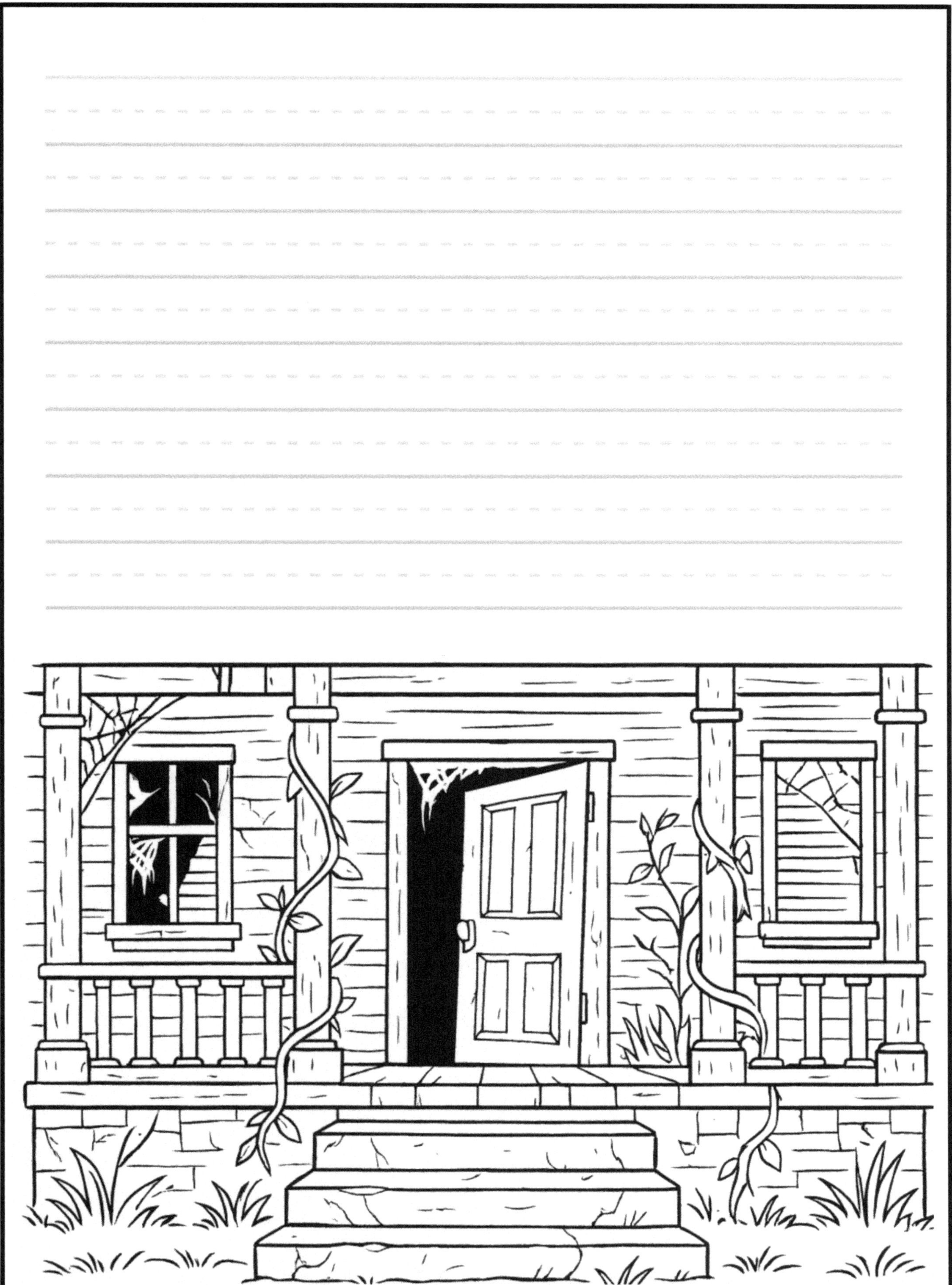

Haunted Mirror

Some spooky tales tell of mirrors that show more than just your reflection. Sometimes they reveal strange faces—or even hidden worlds!

- What would you do if you looked in the mirror and saw a strange person or creature?
- Imagine a mirror that shows a magical land. What would you see there?

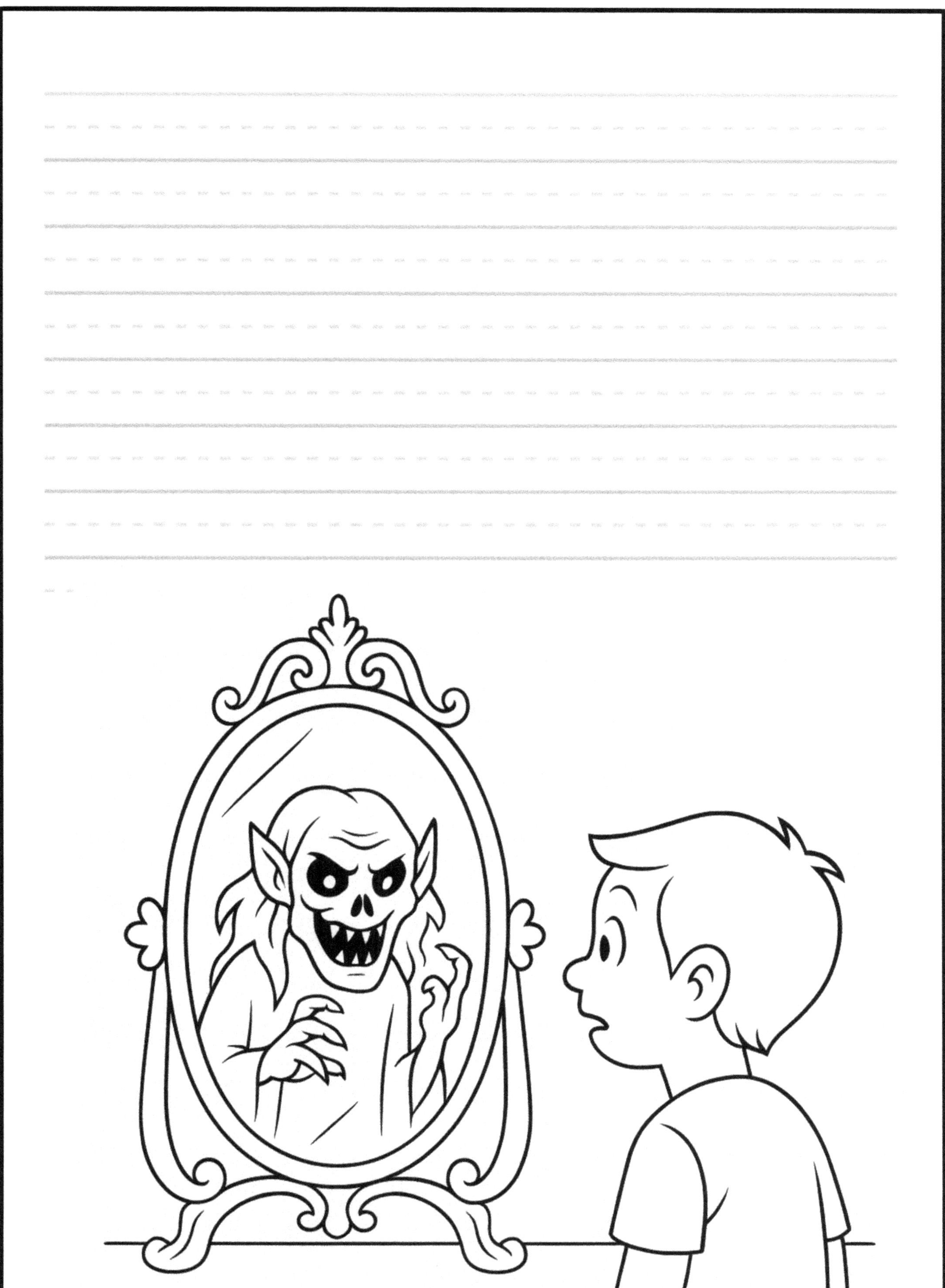

Vultures

Some people think vultures are scary, but vultures are actually very helpful. They clean up the environment by eating dead animals, which helps prevent the spread of disease.

- Do you think vultures are spooky, silly, or cool?
- Would you like to have vultures in your neighborhood? Why?

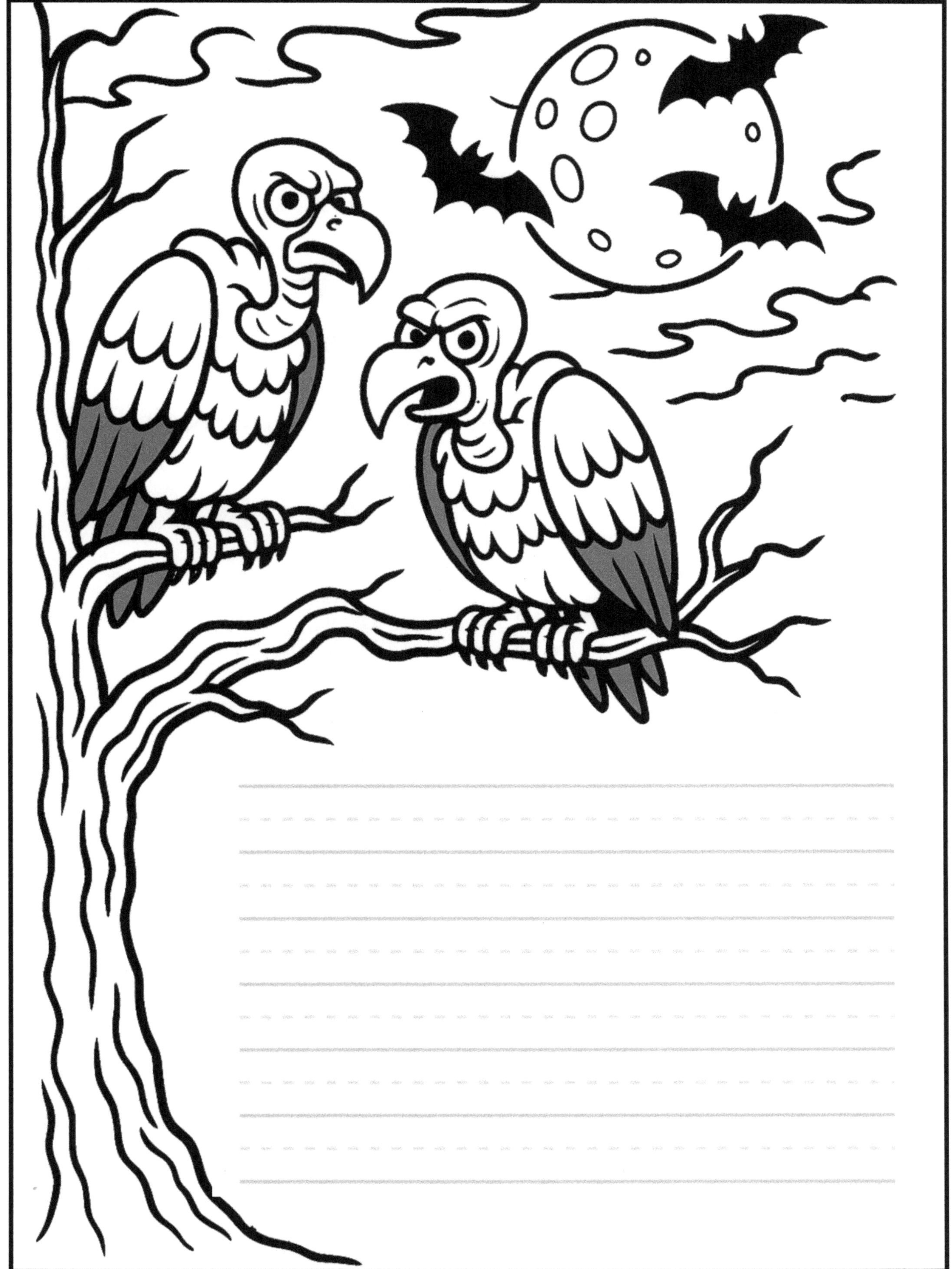

Wizard and Potions

In stories, wizards often keep recipe books of secret mixtures. Some potions make you invisible, let you fly, or even turn you into an animal!

- Make up your own potion recipe. What would it do?
- Write or tell a story about a wizard who accidentally mixes up the wrong potion.

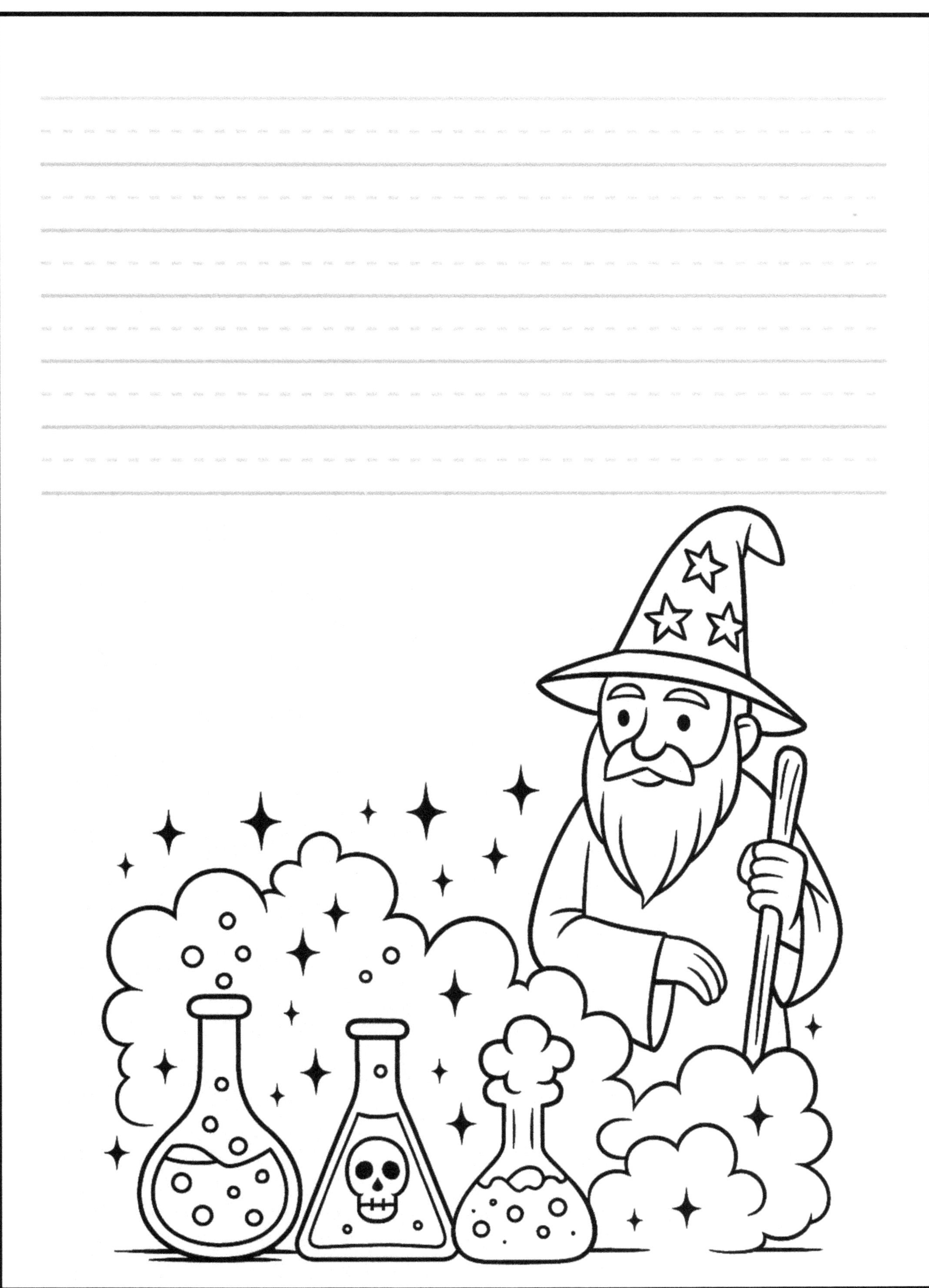

Ghostly Graveyard

In Halloween stories, graveyards are often spooky places with ghosts and zombies and skeletons. But in real life, graveyards are usually places of peace and memory.

- Do you think this ghost looks scary or friendly?
- Write a story about a ghost who helps someone find something they lost.

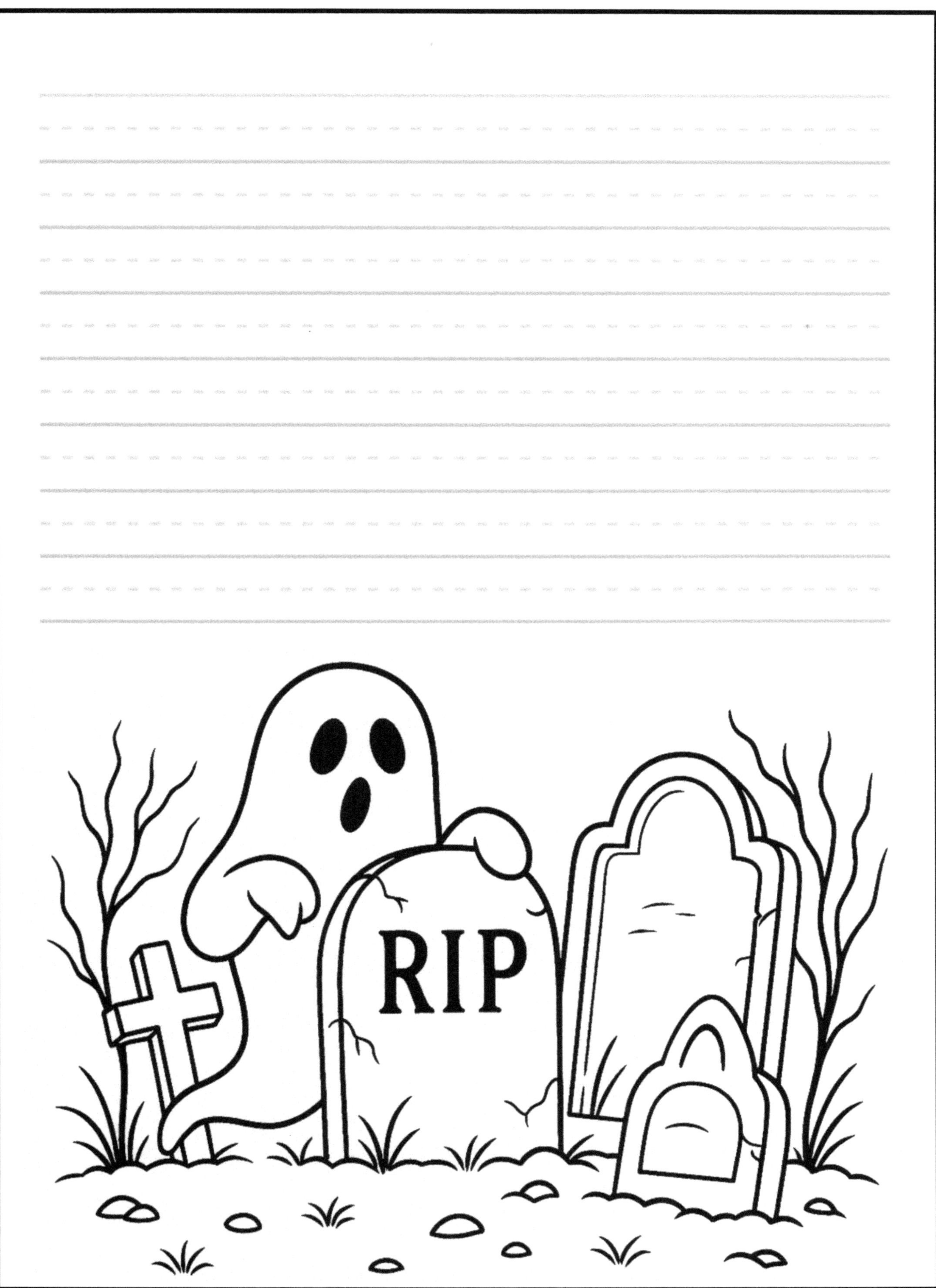

Superheroes

Superheroes have been around for almost 100 years. Early superheroes were comic book characters like Superman and Wonder Woman. On Halloween, many kids and adults dress up as superheroes.

- If you dressed up as a superhero, who would you be?
- What superpower would you like to have? How would you use it?

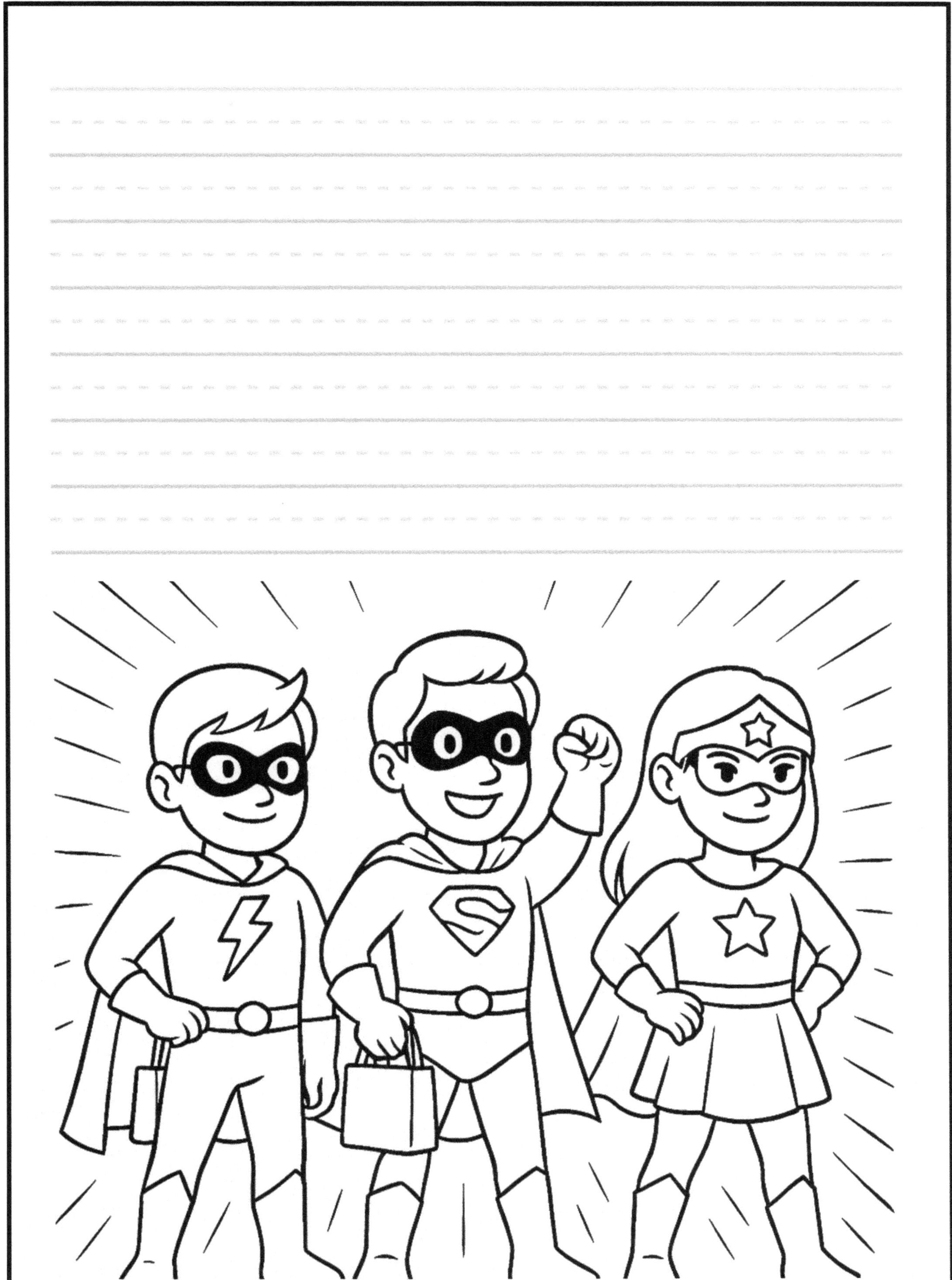

Masks

Long ago, people wore masks during festivals to frighten away evil spirits. Today, masks are often worn for fun—especially on Halloween.

- If you could design your own mask, what would it look like?
- How do you feel when you're wearing a mask?

RENT-A-MASK

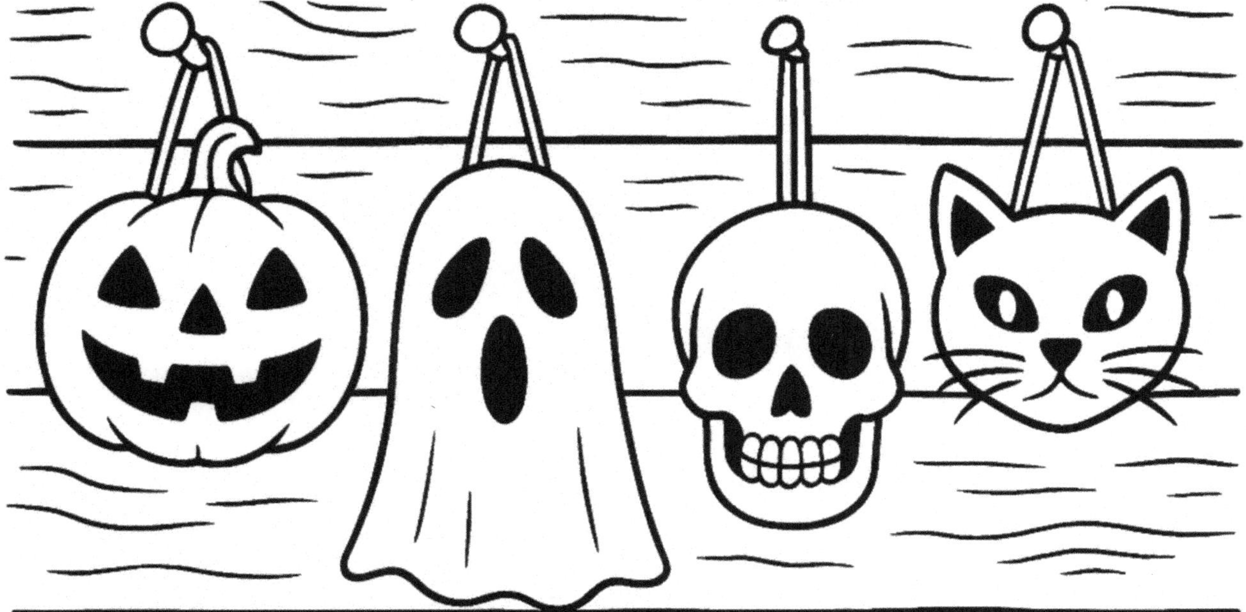

Haunted Tree

Halloween stories often use twisted trees to set a spooky scene. In real life, old twisted trees sometimes do look spooky, especially on a foggy night.

- If you saw a tree that looked like it had a face, what would you think?
- Draw or describe your own spooky tree. Does it move or talk?

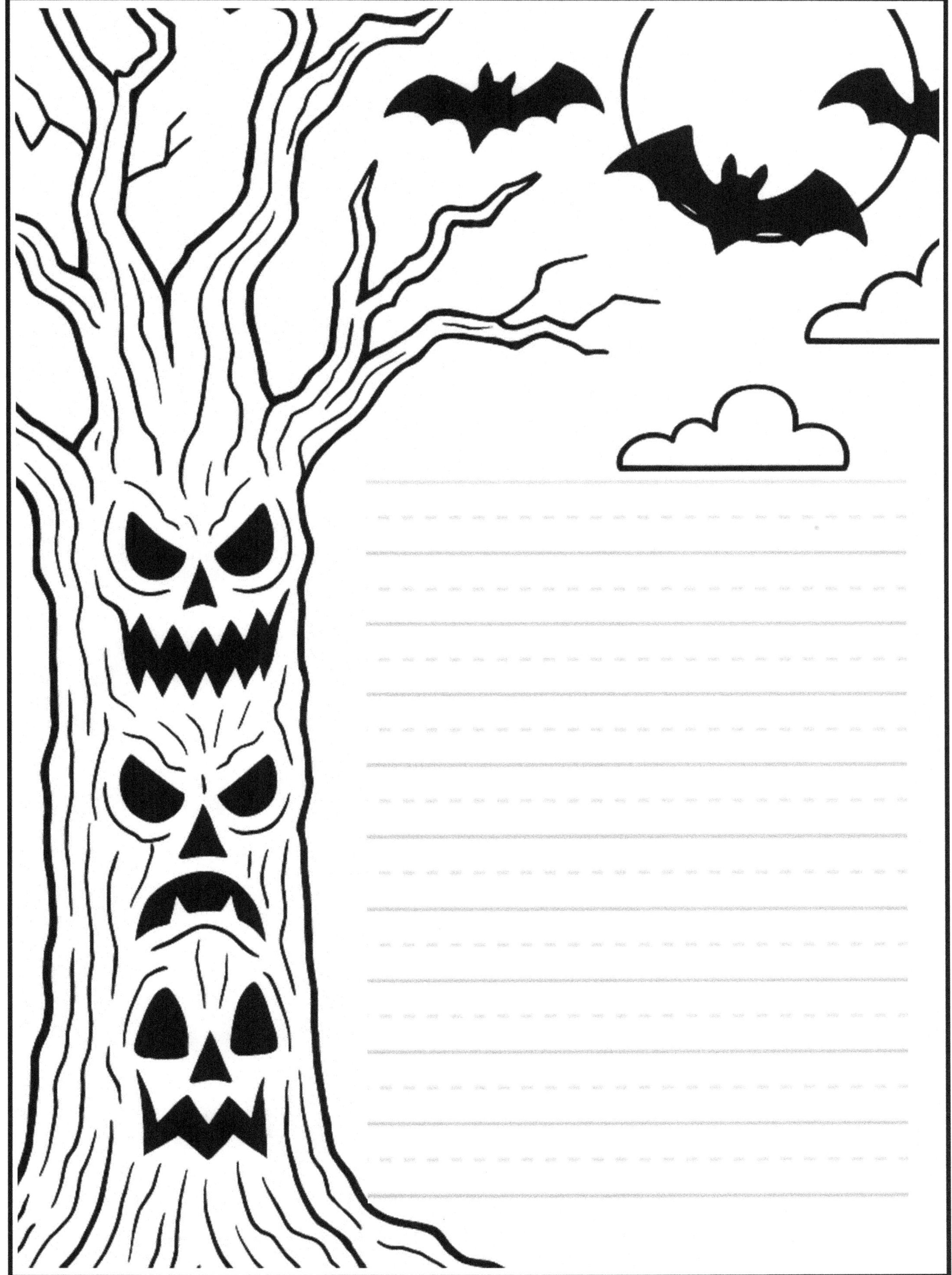

Ghost Stories

People have been telling ghost stories for centuries. Good ghost stories use imagination, sound, and surprise to build suspense.

- What kind of story do you think this ghost is reading to the bats?
- Make up your own ghost story.

GHOST
STORIES

Day of the Dead

Skeletons can look scary, but in Mexico they're part of a joyful holiday called the Day of the Dead. It's celebrated the day after Halloween to honor and remember family and friends who have died.

- Would you rather see a spooky skeleton or a skeleton dancing in the street? Why?
- If you could honor someone special in your family, what would you share about them?

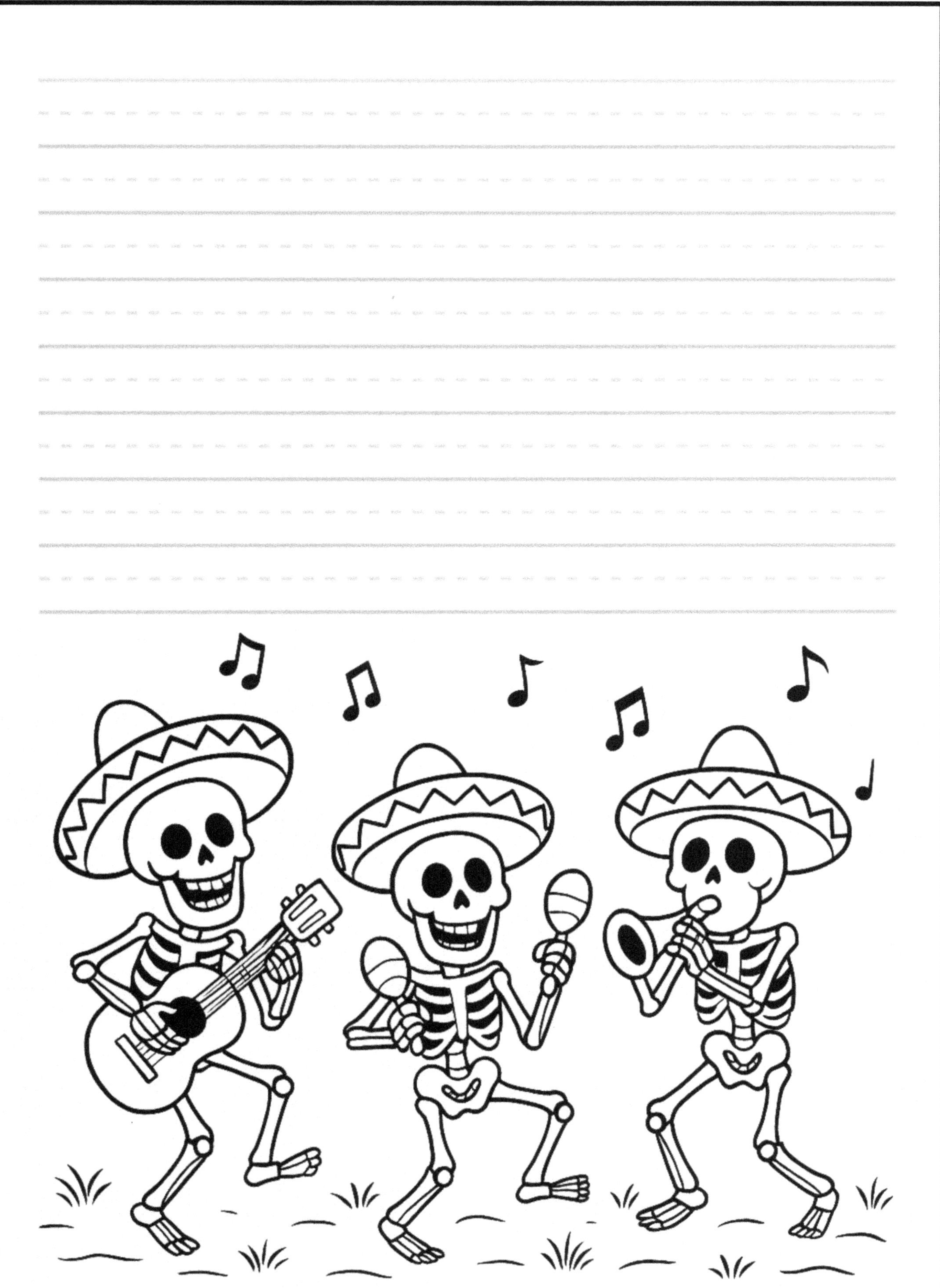

Giant Pumpkin

Pumpkins can grow very fast—up to 50 pounds a day. The world's heaviest pumpkin weighed over 2,700 pounds. That's heavier than a car!

- What would you do if a giant pumpkin grew in your yard?
- Would you like to live inside a giant pumpkin? What would the rooms be like?

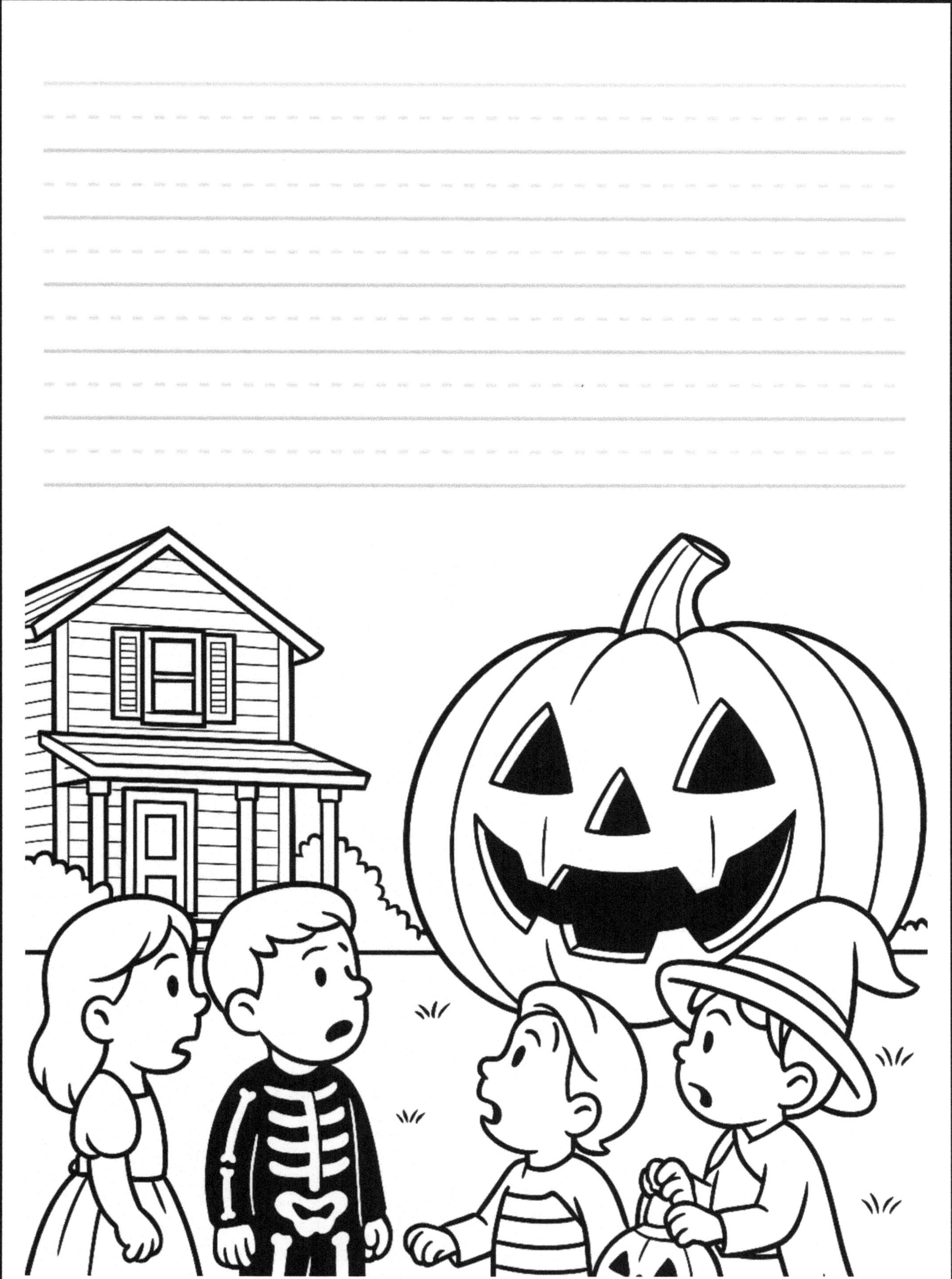

Monsters Trick or Treat

Trick-or-treating became popular in the U.S. almost 100 years ago. On Halloween night, the fun includes all kinds of "monsters"—from imaginary ones to kids dressed in costumes.

- Do you think a monster would wear a Halloween costume?
- Write a story where kids and monsters go trick-or-treating together.

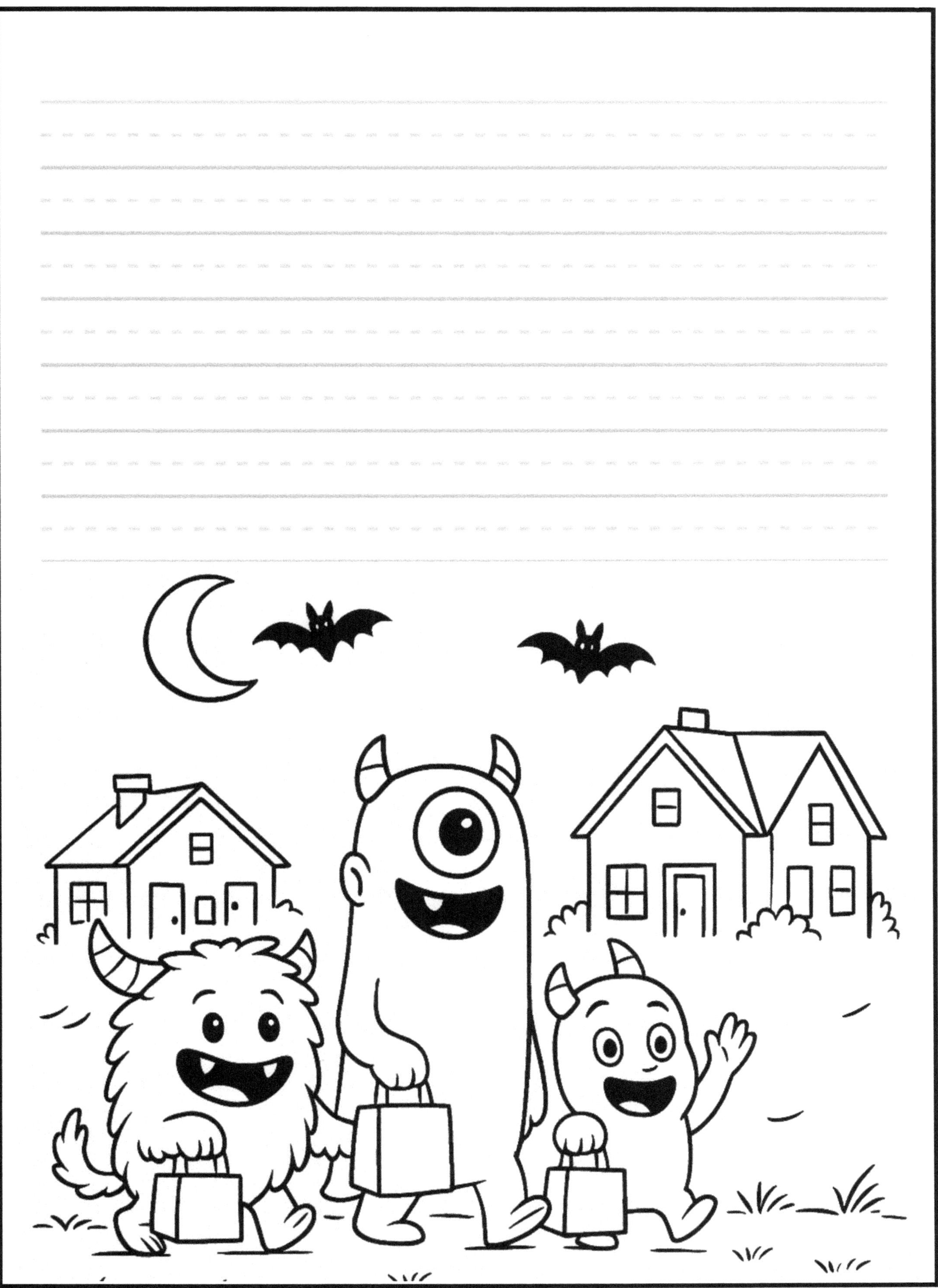

Haunted Town

Some towns claim to be haunted, sometimes because of their tragic history. In stories, haunted towns often have foggy streets, flickering lights, and secret paths.

- Invent a haunted town with a fun name. What makes it special?
- Describe a walking tour of a haunted town with surprise guests!

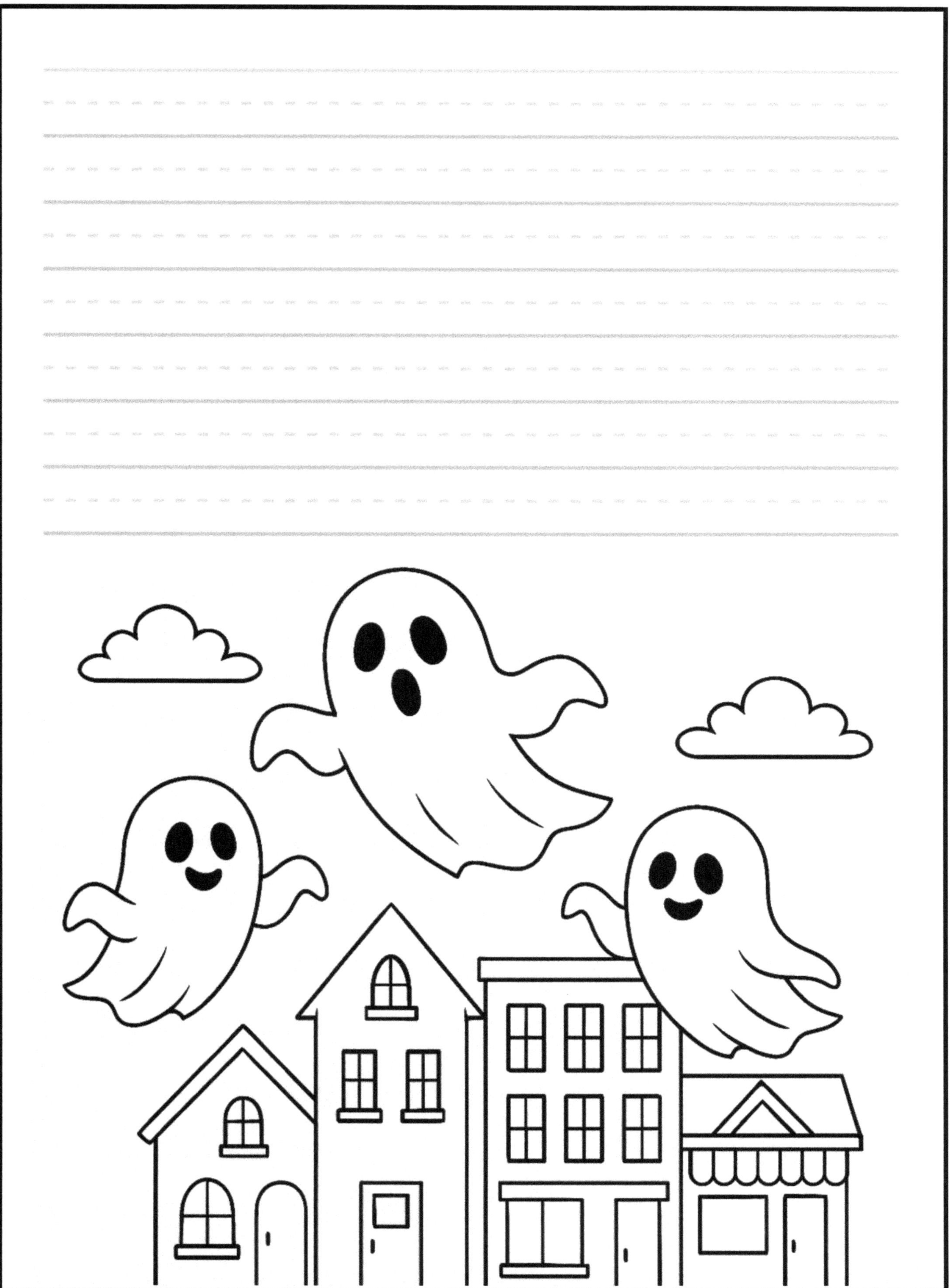

Vampire Family

In legends, vampires were described as very scary creatures. But today, in books, movies, and cartoons, vampires are often shown as stylish—or even silly. Some stories even imagine whole vampire families with funny habits.

- How would you feel if a vampire famiy moved in next door?
- Why do you think people today like to make vampires funny or silly instead of scary?

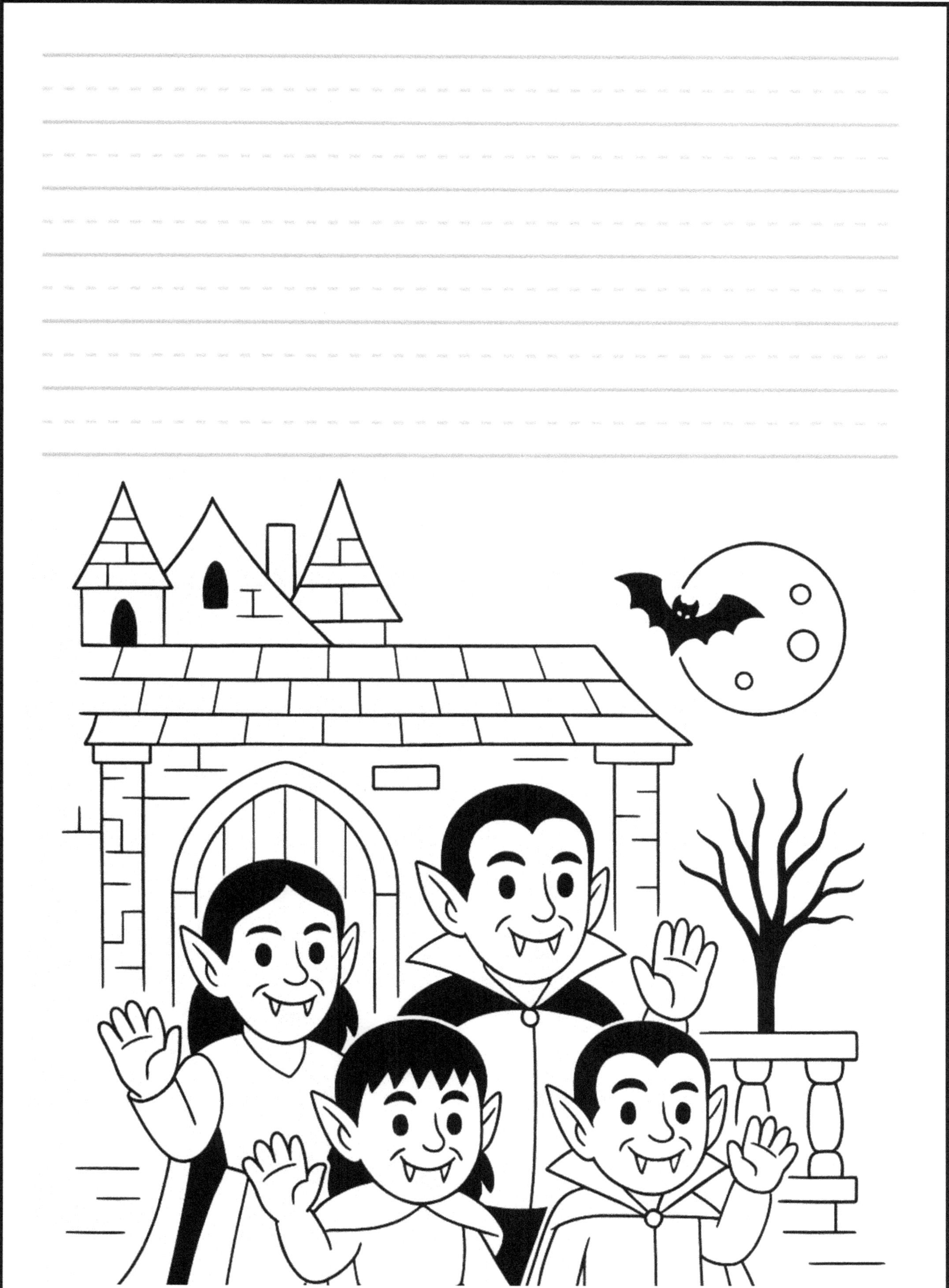

Jack-o'-Lantern

The name jack-o'-lantern comes from an old Irish story about a man called Stingy Jack. He tricked the Devil, and when he died, he had to wander the earth forever. His only light was a glowing coal inside a carved turnip. Over time, people began carving pumpkins instead.

- Design your own funny or spooky jack-o'-lantern. Draw the face on one of the uncarved pumpkins in the picture.
- Imagine each pumpkin in the border has a different story. Pick one and write its story.

Halloween Costumes

Dressing up in costumes has been part of Halloween since the 1500s! Kids today dress up like movie characters, animals, ghosts, monsters, and even food.

- What is your favorite Halloween costume?
- Describe a brand-new costume that's never been seen before.

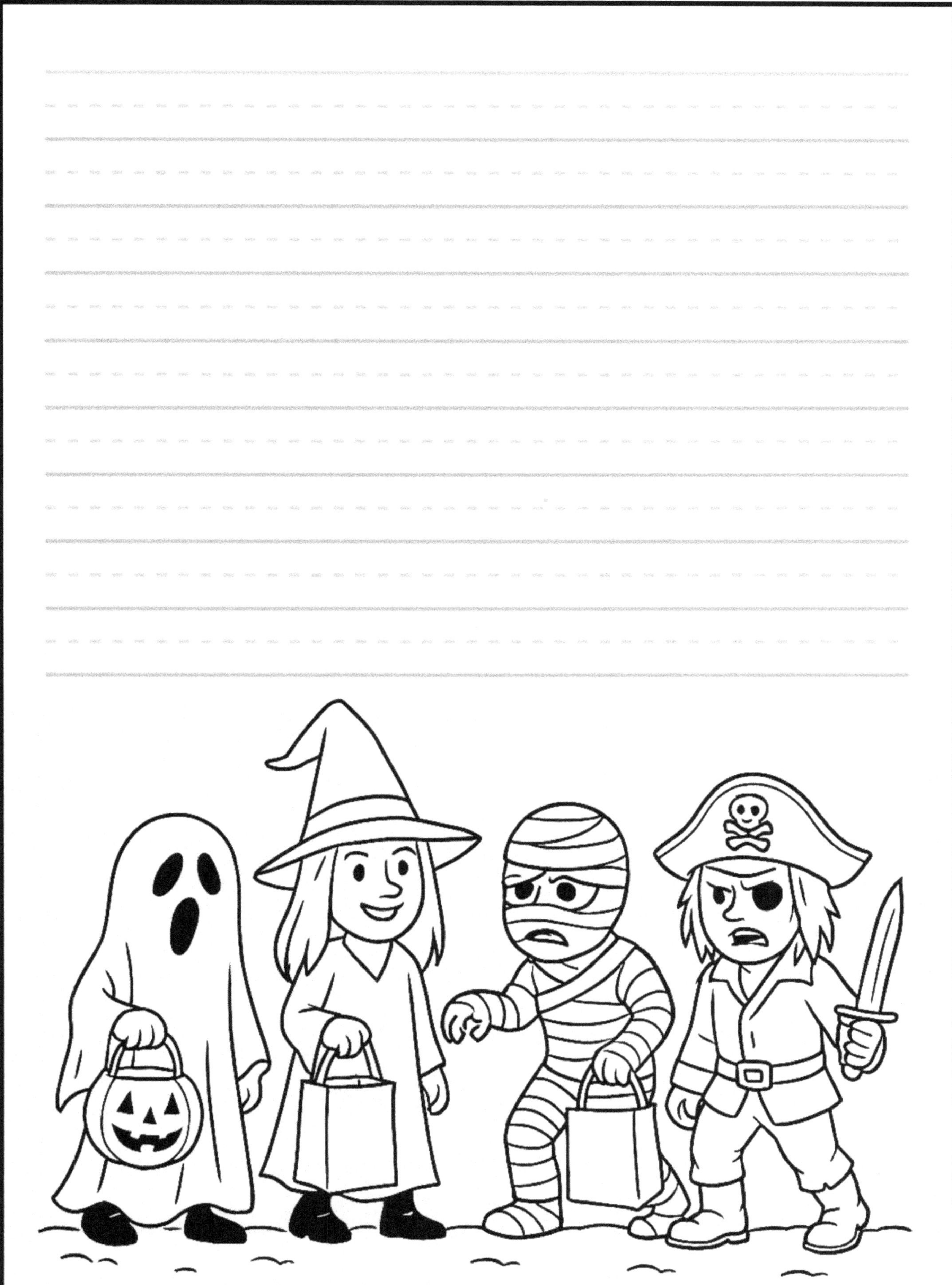

Magic Cat?

Long ago, some people believed witches could change into black cats to sneak around and cast spells. Today, some people still think black cats are unlucky—but others believe they bring extra good luck!

- What kind of spells might a cat create?
- Write a silly or spooky spell using things found at home.

SPELLS

Werewolf

Werewolves are famous creatures in Halloween stories and movies. They are people who magically change into wolves, often under a full moon. In legends, this usually happens after being bitten by another werewolf.

- Would you want to turn into a werewolf? Why or why not?
- What do you think this werewolf is playing on his guitar? Write some funny or spooky lyrics for his song.

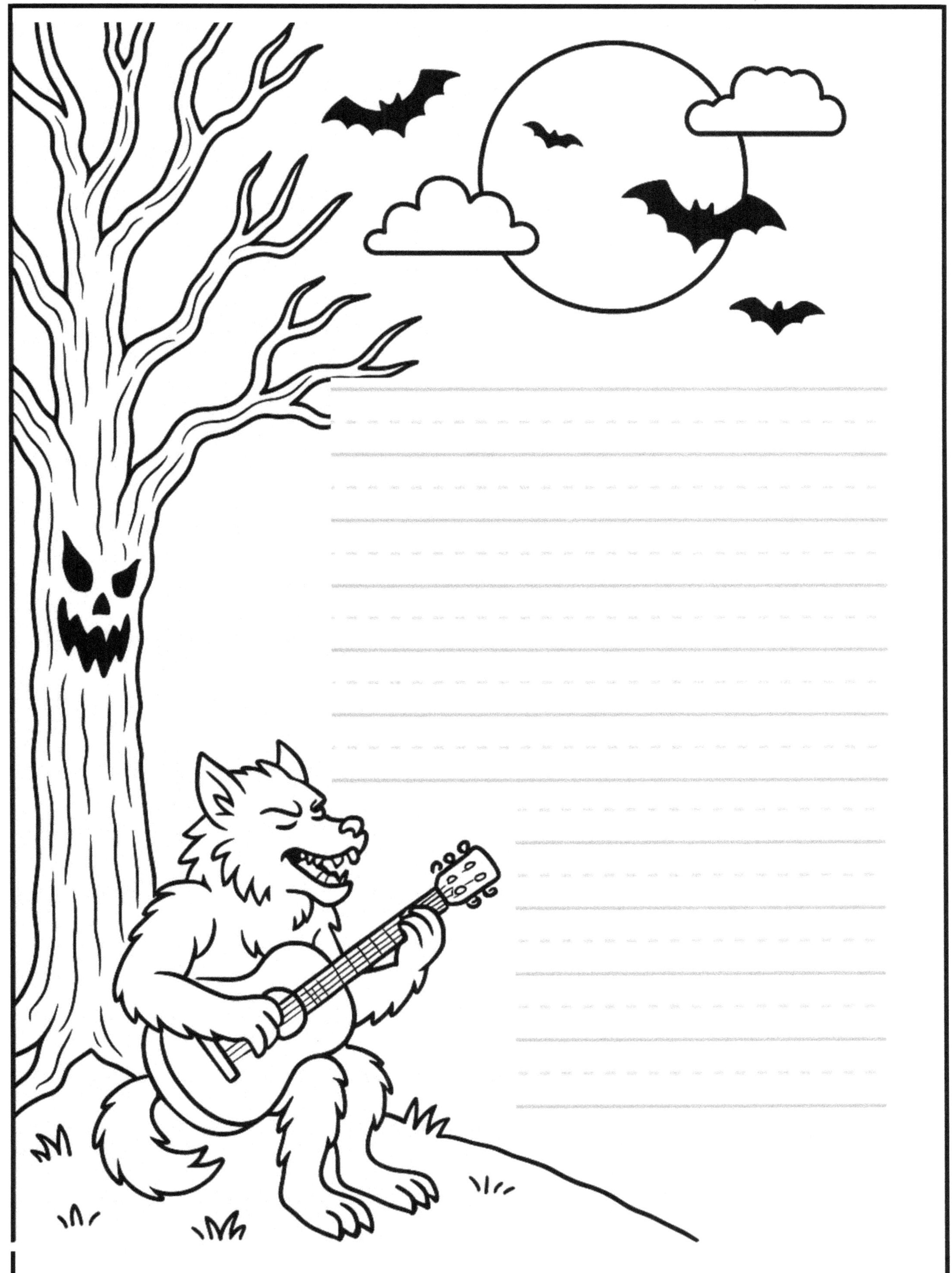

Scarecrow

In stories, scarecrows sometimes come to life and go on adventures. In real life, scarecrows are used by farmers to keep birds away from crops—but clever birds often figure out scarecrows are not real people.

- Why do you think this bird is not afraid of the scarecrow?
- Describe a Halloween where the scarecrows in the field all come alive!

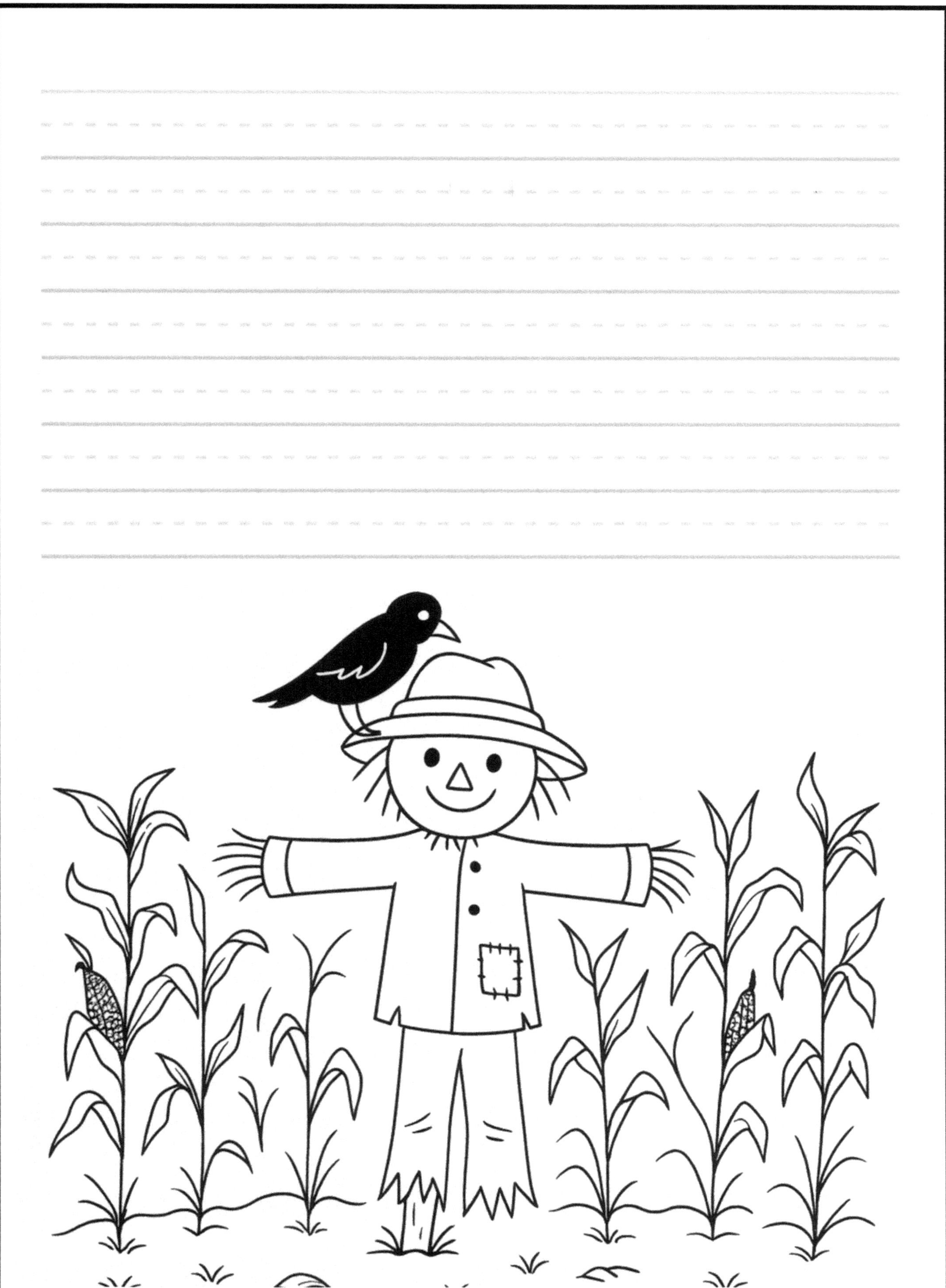

Witches' Brew

In stories, witches stir up bubbling brews in big cauldrons, tossing in things like dragon scales or frog toes. Long ago, though, "witches' brews" were often made from herbs—and some of them really worked as medicine!

- Would you drink a brew if you didn't know what was in it? Why or why not?
- Write a recipe for a brew that could make someone feel healthy and strong.

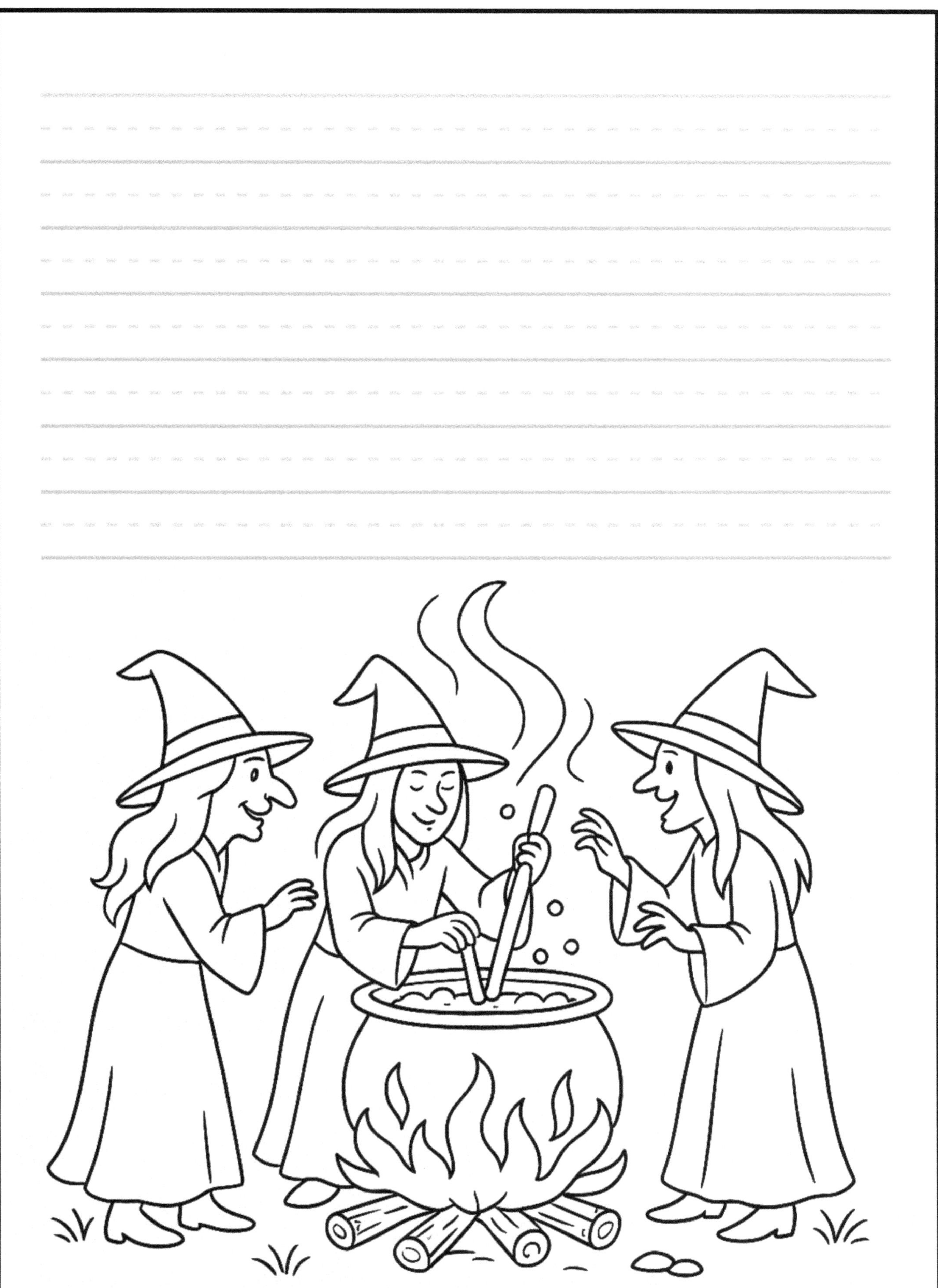

Monster Mash

Monsters with goofy faces and wild colors make Halloween feel silly and fun instead of scary. Drawing monsters is a great way to use your imagination and creativity.

- Which monster in the border is your favorite? Why?
- Invent your own monster. Is it scary or friendly? What does your monster do on Halloween?

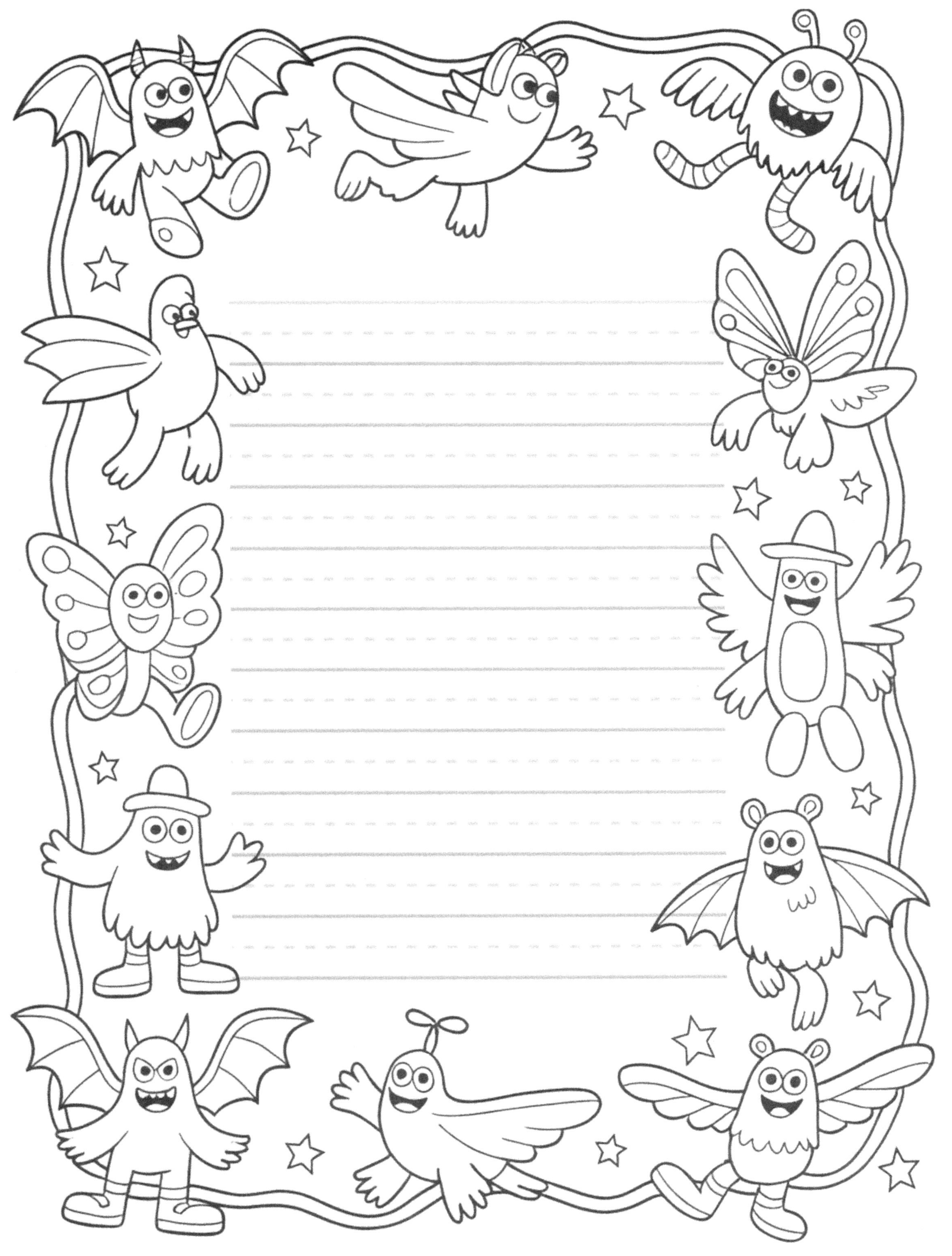

Mummy Soccer

Real mummies are preserved bodies from ancient Egypt. Halloween mummies are usually kids wrapped in bandages for fun.

- How would a mummy play soccer with all those wrappings?
- How long do you think a jack-o'-lantern would last if you used it as a soccer ball?

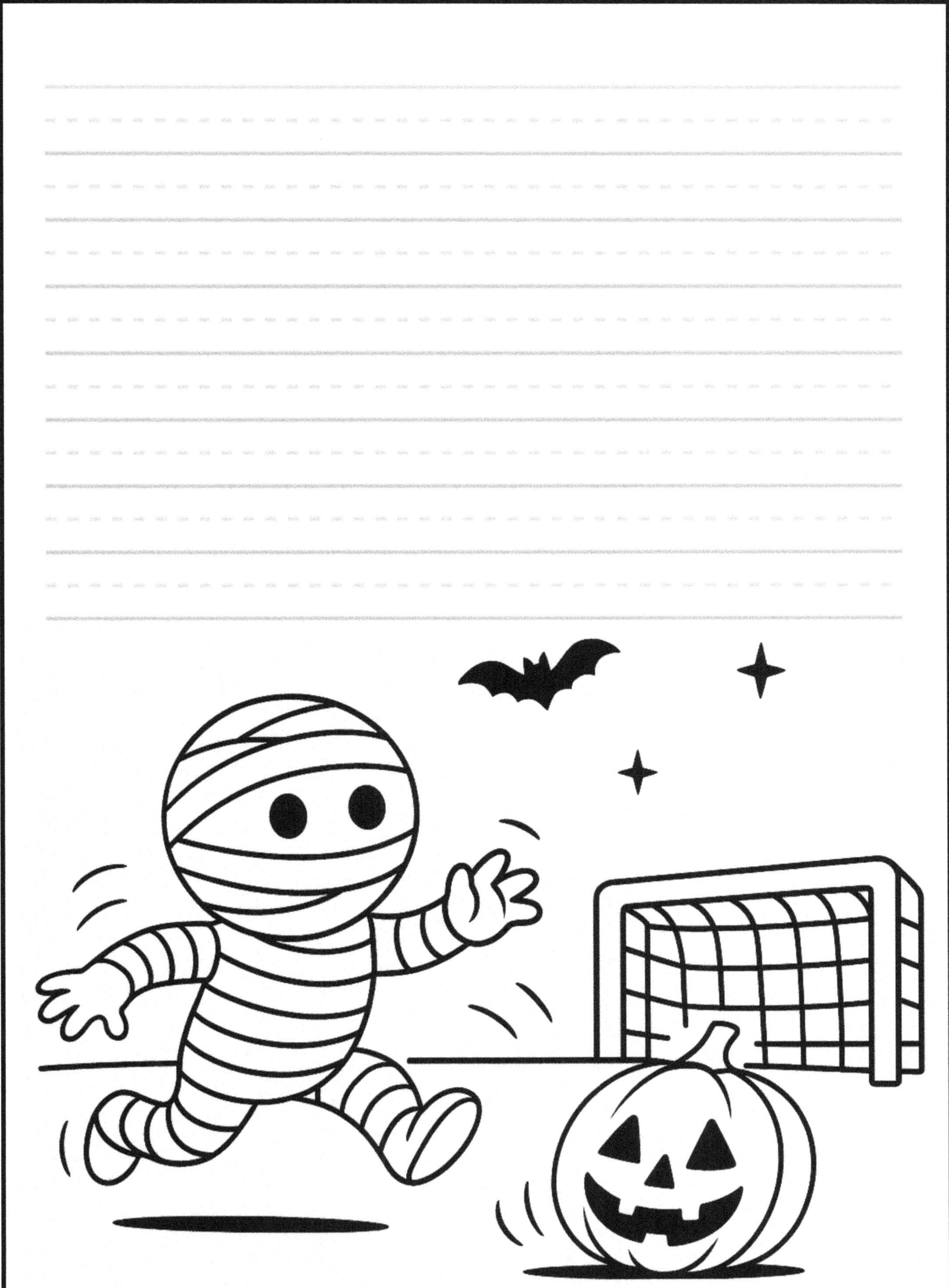

Frankenstein's Monster

Mary Shelley wrote Frankenstein when she was only 18 years old! Frankenstein is the name of the scientist, not the monster. In many versions of the story, the monster is actually kind but misunderstood.

- What would you do if Frankenstein's monster moved in next door?
- Do you think this monster wants to make friends? Why or why not?

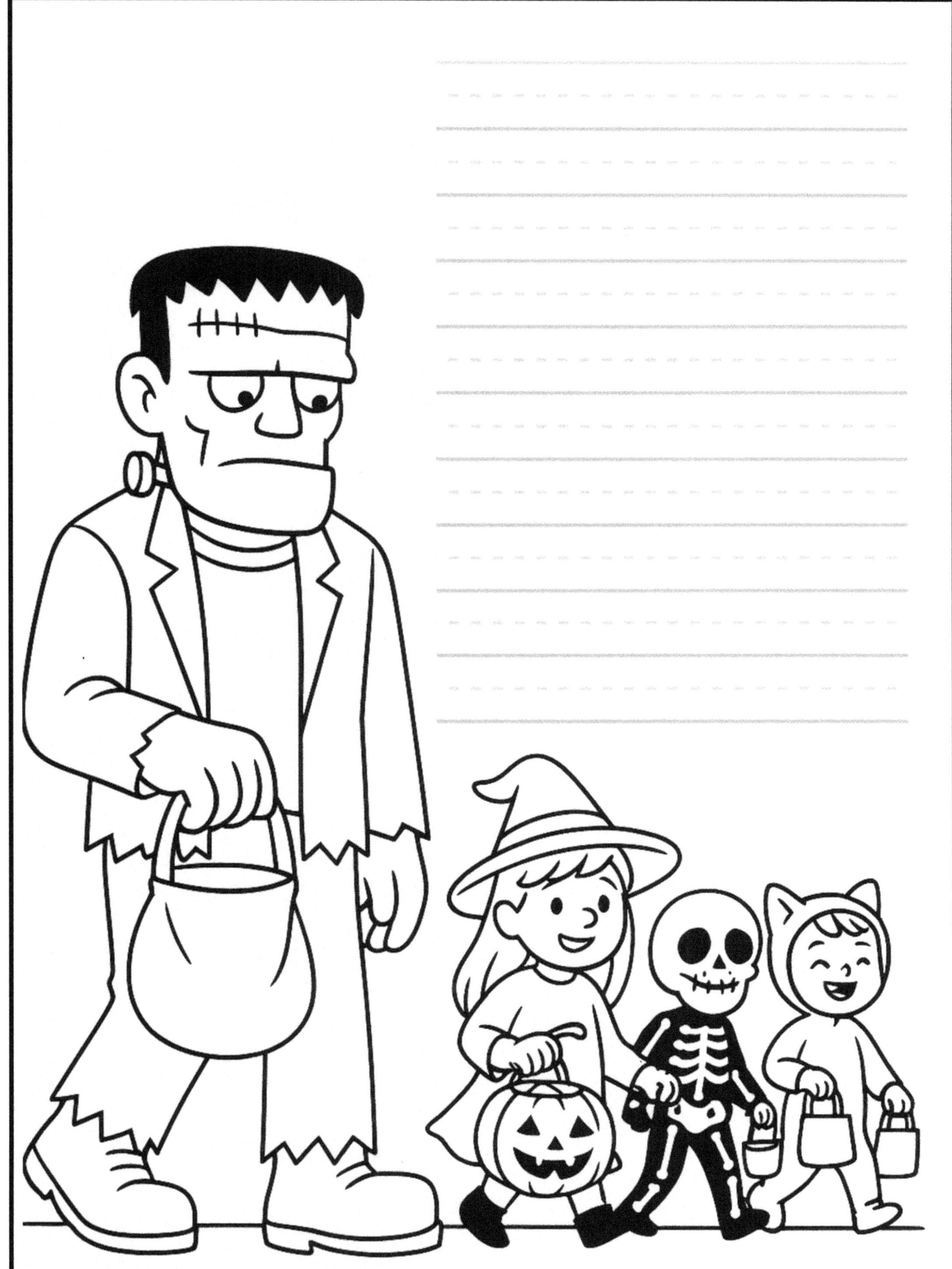

Monster Footprints

Huge footprints are often used in movies to show a monster is nearby. Some people even make fake monster tracks in the snow or dirt for fun.

- Where do you think these monster footprints lead?
- Write or tell a detective story about following these tracks to solve a mystery.

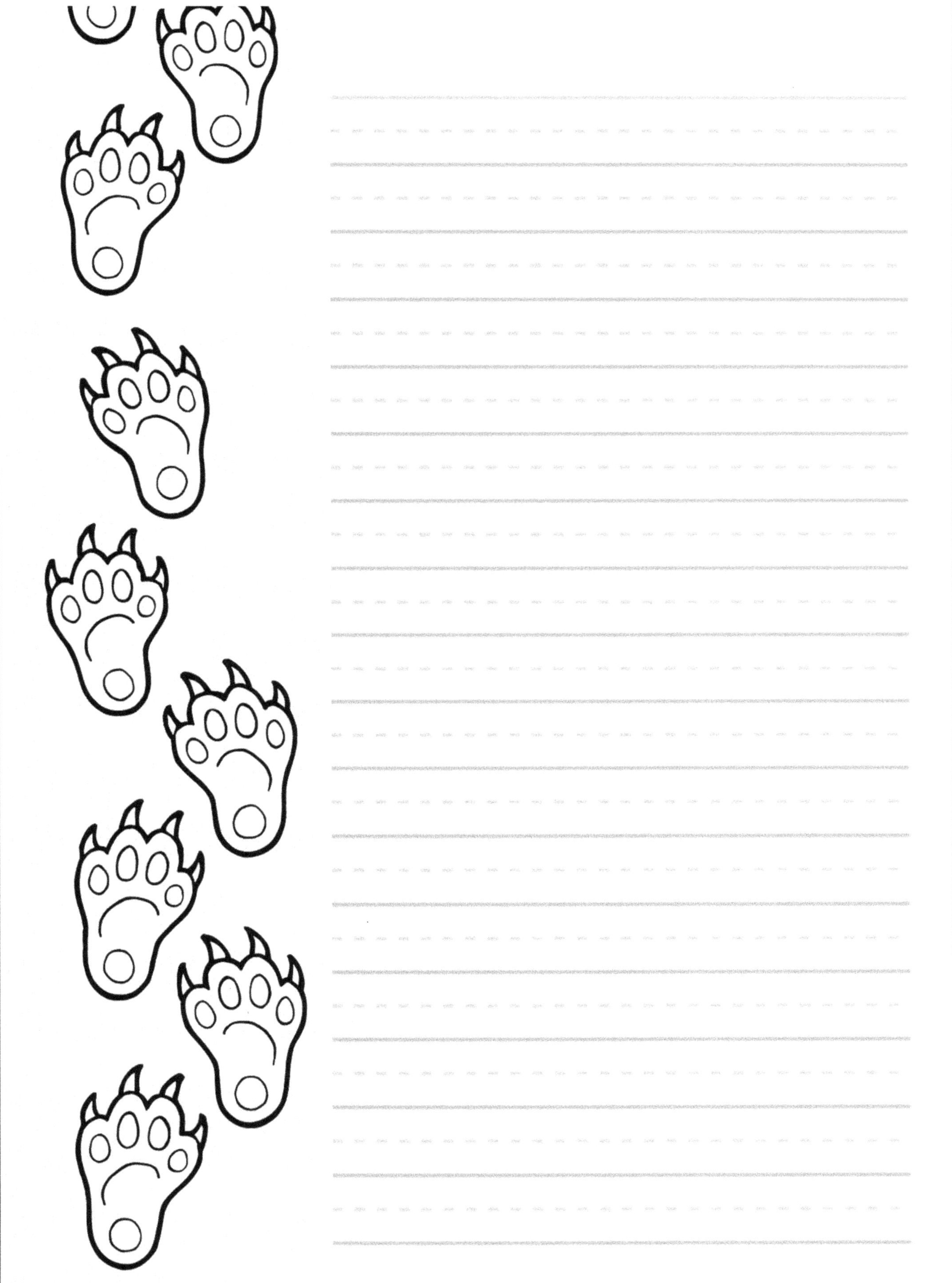

Ghostly Treehouse

Treehouses are a place for imagination and adventure—perfect for ghostly visitors. In stories, ghosts often come back to places where they once had fun or made special memories.

- What would it be like to meet a friendly ghost who lives in your treehouse?
- Write about a group of kids who discover a haunted treehouse with a surprise inside.

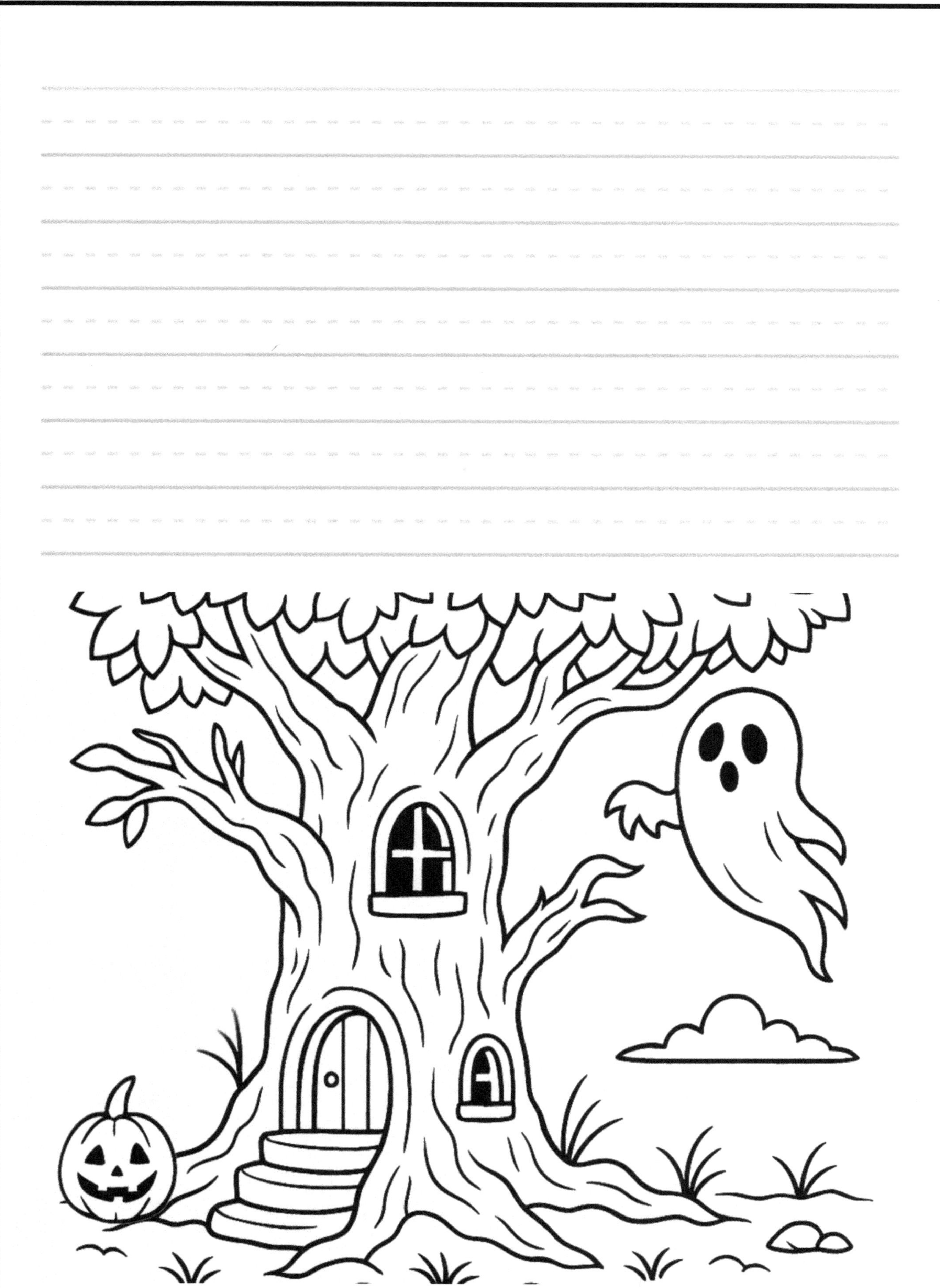

Pumpkin Stack

Pumpkins come in many shapes and sizes. Some pumpkins weigh hundreds of pounds, while others are small enough to fit in your hand. Stacking them into towers is a popular fall decoration.

- What would you do to keep your pumpkin stack from falling over and rolling away?
- What kind of pumpkin stack would you design to win a Halloween decoration contest?

Haunted Library

Libraries are great settings for spooky stories, full of old books and mysterious corners. Some real libraries are thought to be haunted—often by former librarians or famous authors!

- What kind of ghost might haunt a library? What books would it read?
- Imagine you find a secret passage behind a bookshelf. What do you think you will find?

Flying School

In folklore, witches often fly on broomsticks. Some modern stories imagine witches going to school to learn flying and other magical skills.

- Write a report card for a witch who is learning to fly. What special skills would you grade?
- Imagine yourself learning to fly. Describe your first adventure.

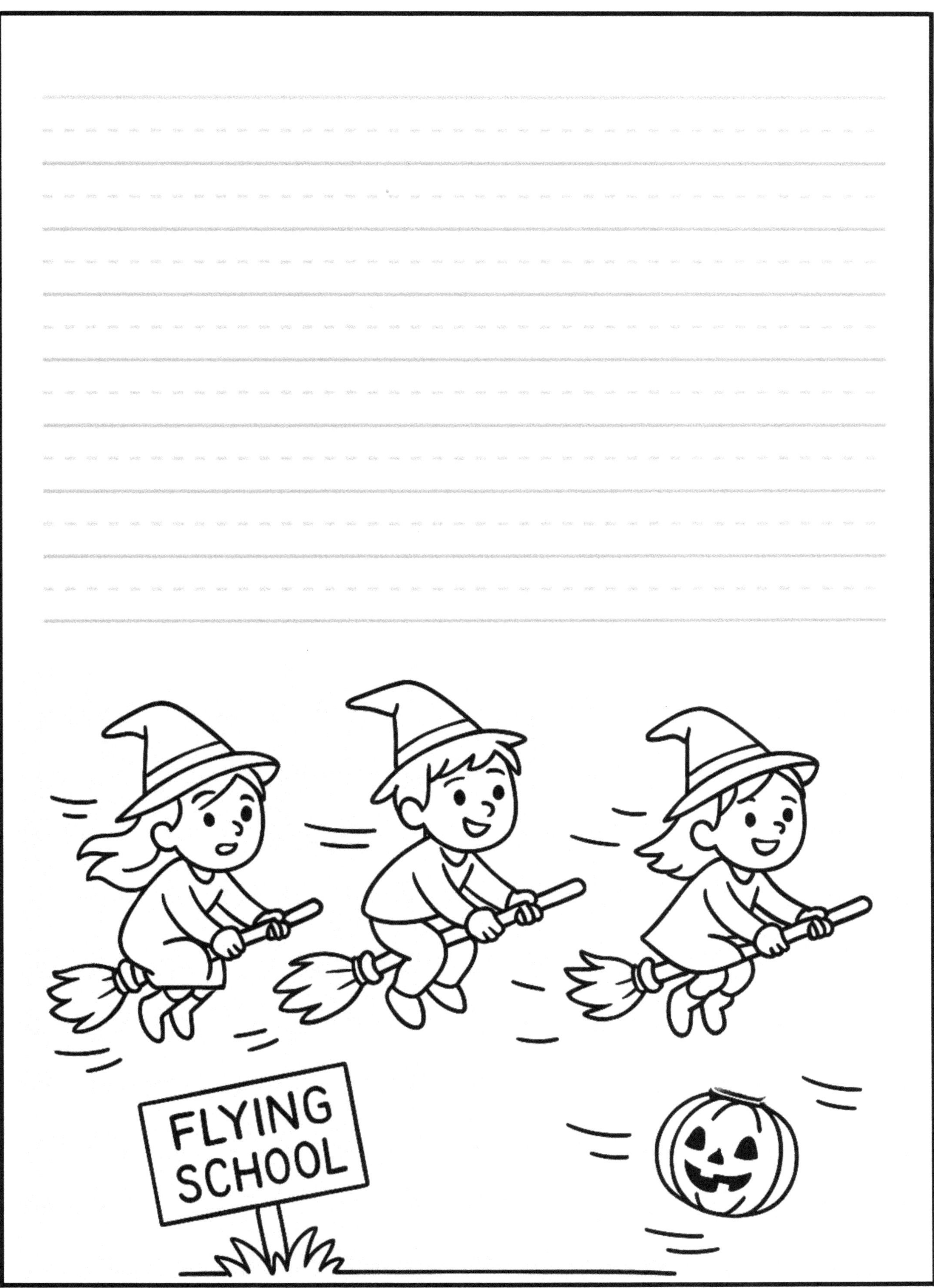

FLYING
SCHOOL

Creepy Snakes

Snakes are often used in magical stories because they are mysterious. In some myths, snakes are protectors. In others, they are tricksters or symbols of change and growth.

- Imagine a magical snake—what powers does it have?
- Write a story about a snake who sneaks into a Halloween party.

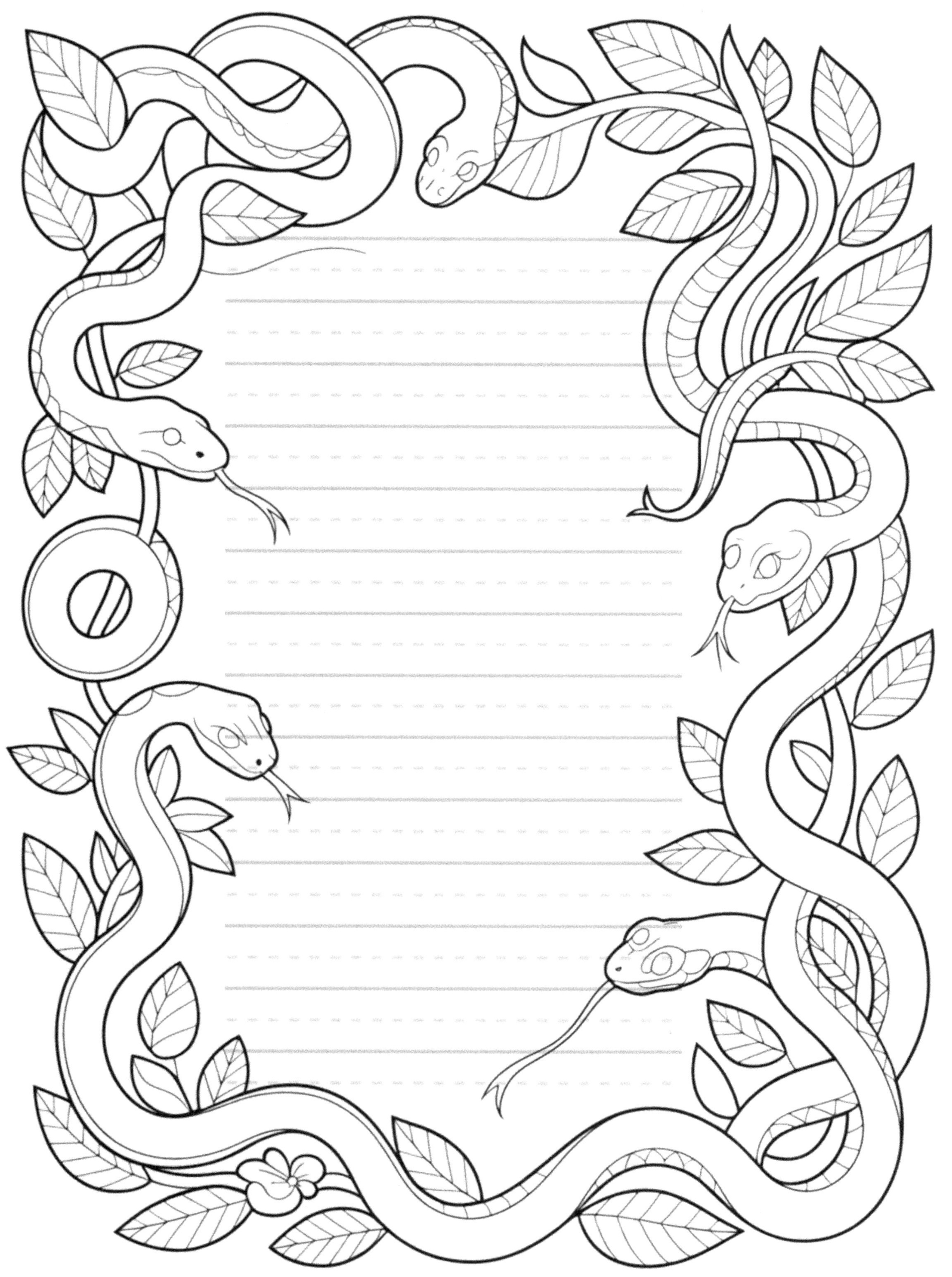

Haunted Attic

Attics are often filled with old treasures—and spooky shadows! In stories, attics are a favorite hiding place for ghosts who make mysterious noises.

- Describe an attic where each box holds something magical.
- Write a story called "The Whisper in the Attic."

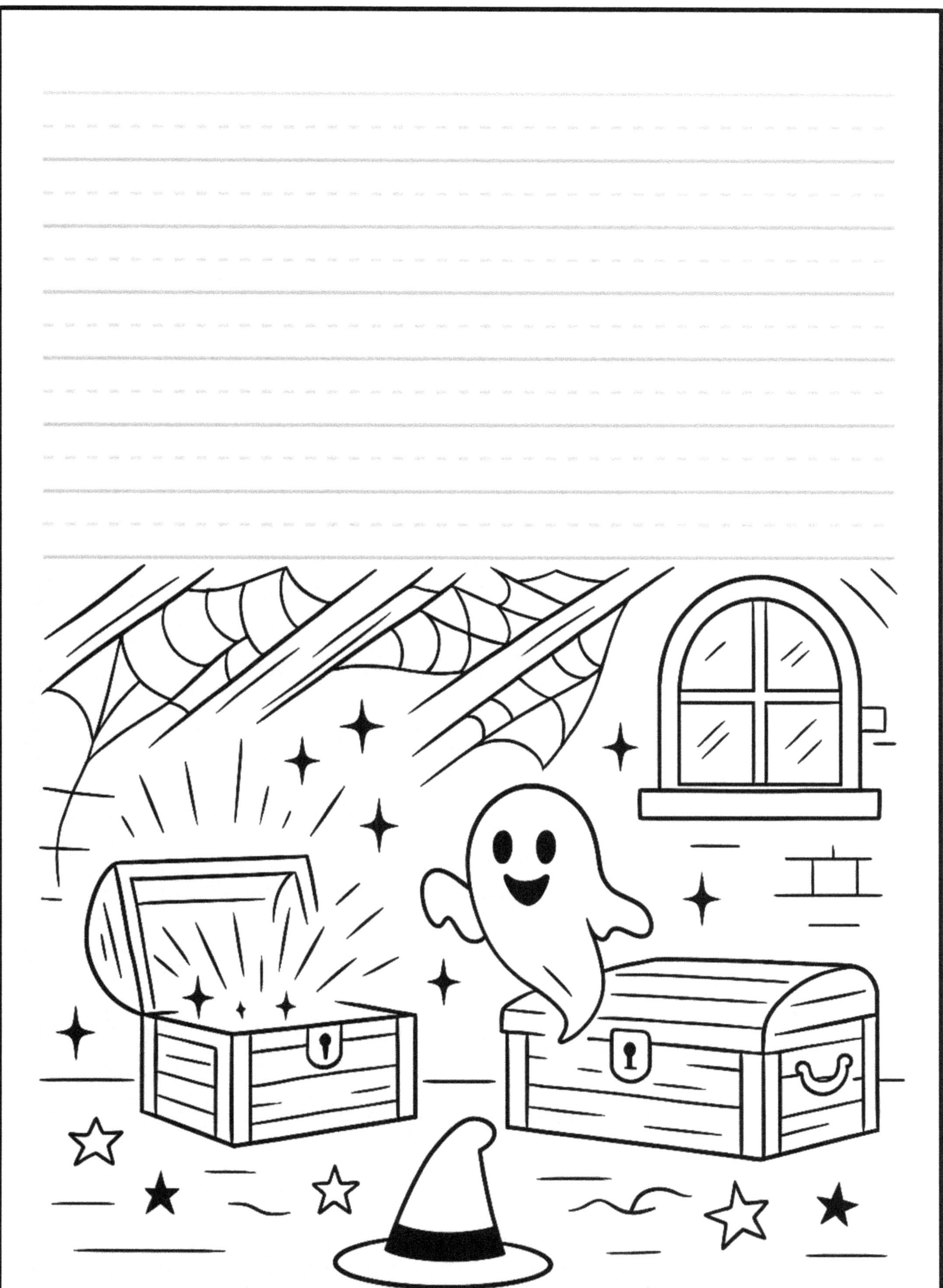

Vampire at the Organ

In old movies, vampires are often shown playing pipe organs in spooky castles. That's because the pipe organ is one of the oldest and most dramatic instruments, perfect for creepy music!

- What kind of music do you think a vampire likes to play?
- Write or tell about a vampire performing at a Halloween talent show.

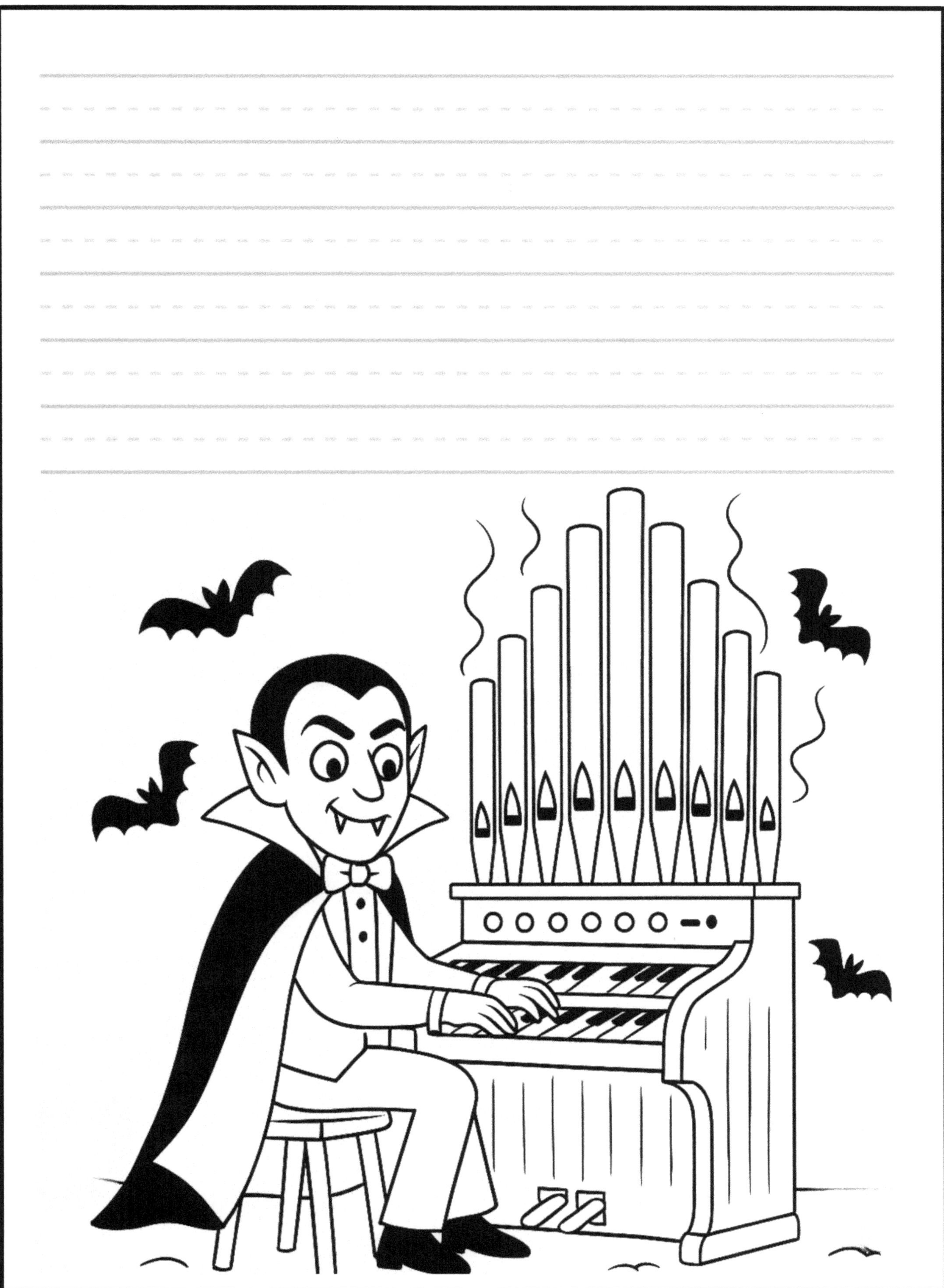

Magic Brooms

In legends, witches' brooms aren't just for flying—they sometimes have magic of their own. Some stories imagine brooms that can think, talk, or act in funny ways.

- What do you think makes each of these brooms special?
- Write an ad for the "Broom of the Future". What features does it have?

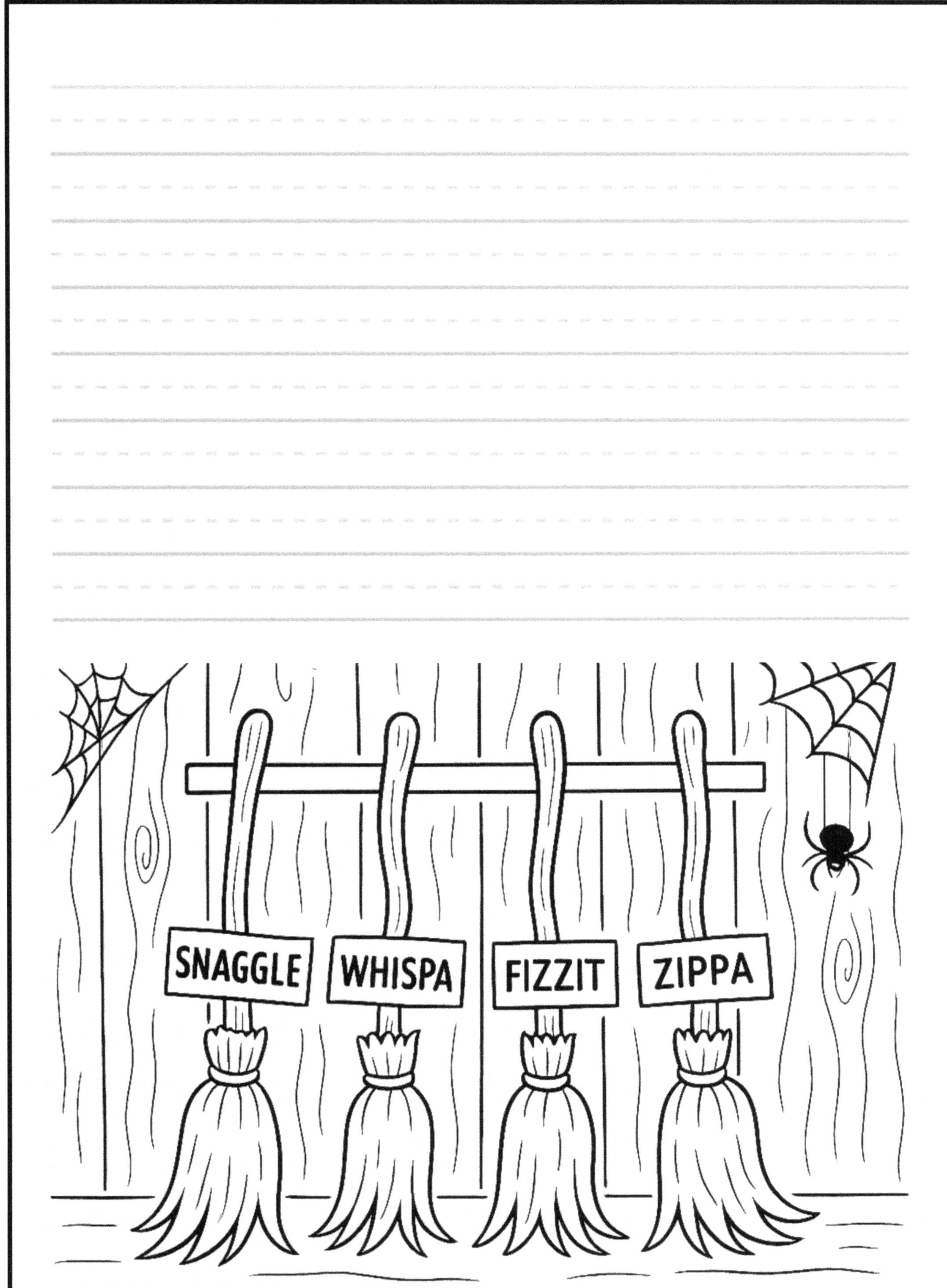

SNAGGLE
WHISPA
FIZZIT
ZIPPA

Haunted Carnival

Carnivals can be fun... or mysterious! In Halloween stories, carnival tents are sometimes haunted. When you go inside, you might find spooky clowns, mirrors, and strange surprises.

- What do you think you would you find inside this haunted carnival tent?
- Write a story about a Halloween carnival with magical prizes.

Gargoyle

Gargoyles are stone statues often seen on old buildings. They were shaped so rainwater could pour out of their mouths instead of dripping down the walls. In folklore, gargoyles were said to scare away evil spirits and come to life at night.

- Write a story about a gargoyle that comes to life for just one Halloween night.
- Imagine you are a gargoyle. What do you think about the Halloween celebrations and noise below?

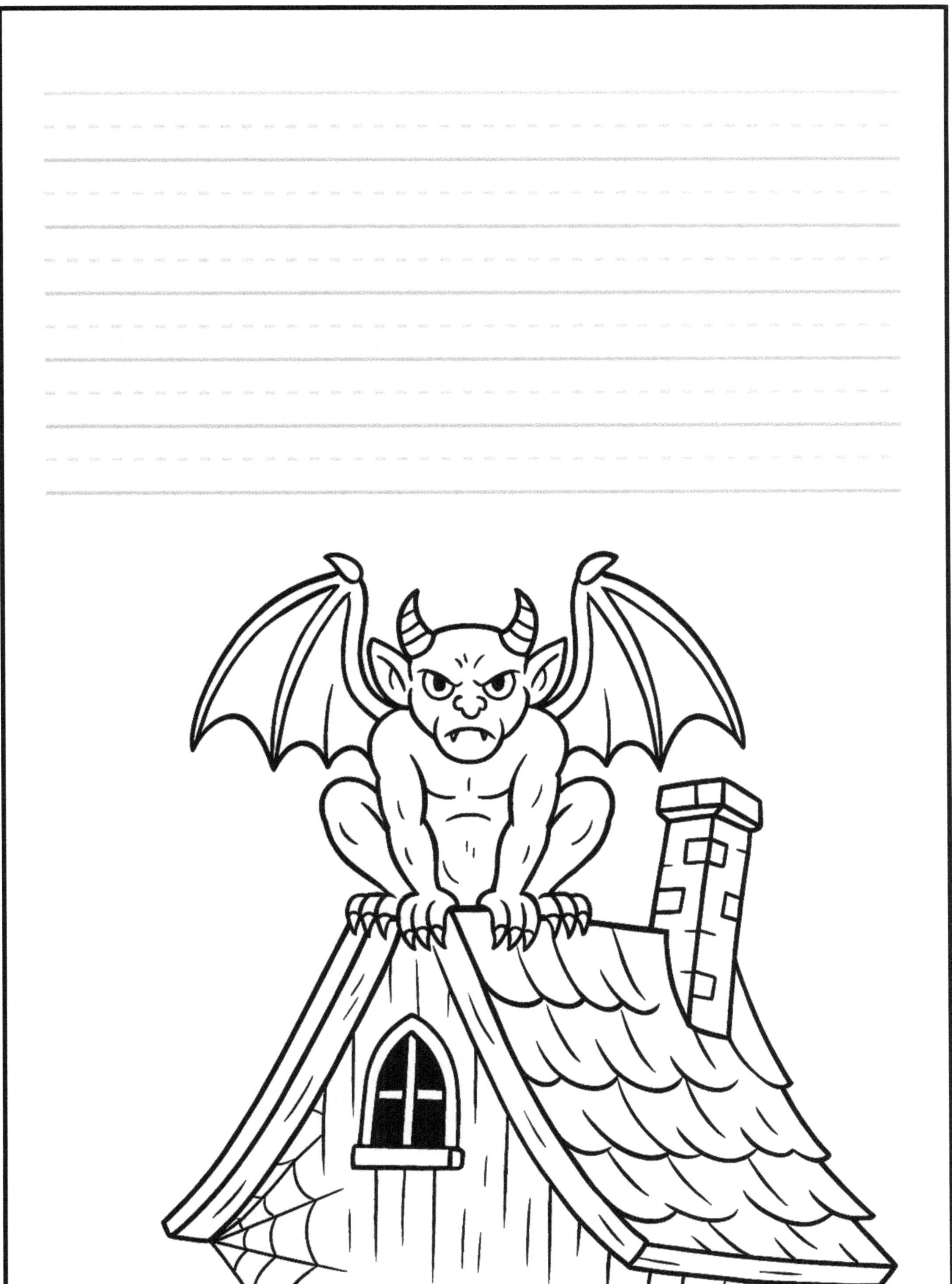

Haunted Castle

Castles are old stone buildings that were once used by kings, queens, and knights. In spooky stories, haunted castles are said to be filled with ghosts, bats, and strange sounds.

- Imagine you are exploring this castle. What do you find behind the big doors?
- If you met one of the castle ghosts, would it be scary, silly, or friendly? What would you do together?

Glenwood Treehouse

Kids (and some adults) have built forts and hideouts for centuries. Treehouses are great for hanging out with friends, reading and telling stories, and just getting away from it all.

- Would you feel safe or scared in this treehouse on Halloween night? Why?
- If you could have any hideout, fort, or treehouse you wanted, what would you choose?

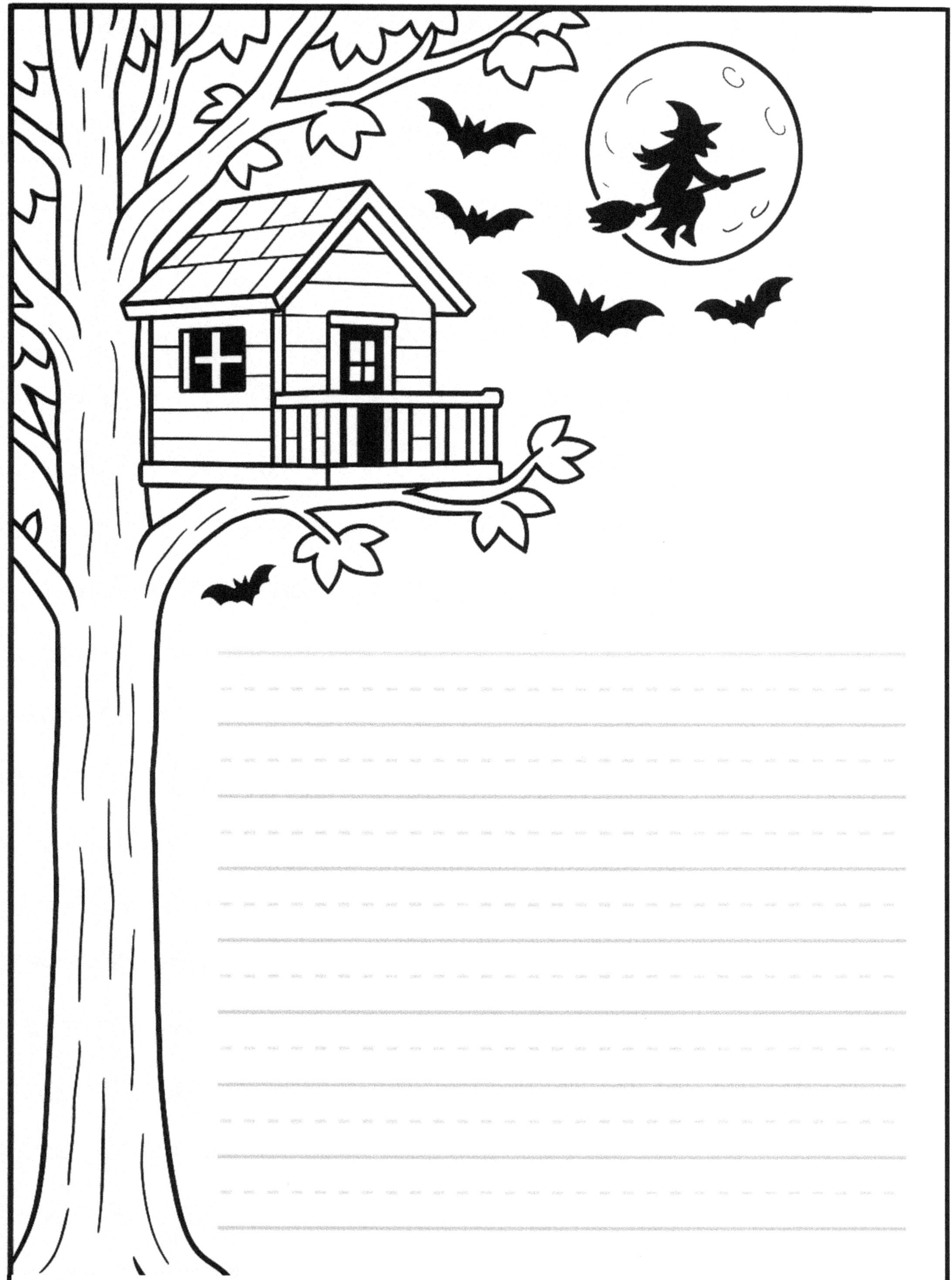

Why Handwriting and Art Matter

Peggy Healy Stearns, Ph.D.

Handwriting and coloring might seem like simple childhood activities—but they're powerful tools for learning, growth, and self-expression. Here are some ways these activities support brain development, emotional well-being, and academic skills.

Handwriting Builds Brains

In our digital world, it's easy to think handwriting is old-fashioned—something to phase out in favor of typing, tapping, and swiping. But when it comes to young children, the research tells a different story.

Learning to write by hand is about way more than putting letters on a page. It's a powerful brain-building tool that helps kids become better readers, thinkers, and learners. Here's what handwriting actually does for a child's growing brain—and why it's so worthwhile.

Handwriting Lights Up the Brain

When kids write letters by hand, they're not just practicing motor skills—they're lighting up multiple areas of the brain at once. Scientists using brain scans (like fMRIs) have found that handwriting activates regions tied to memory, language, and visual processing—far more than typing on a keyboard does.

That's because handwriting is a complex task. It involves planning, fine motor control, visual attention, and physical movement—all working together. This 'whole brain' experience strengthens important neural connections, laying a solid foundation for learning.

It Boosts Letter Recognition and Reading

When a child writes a letter by hand—over and over again—the brain begins to recognize that letter more quickly. That's because the child has formed a strong mental template for it through both movement and vision.

In contrast, when kids only see letters on a screen or keyboard, their brains don't get that same hands-on learning. Research shows that children who practice handwriting learn letters faster and remember them longer—which is key to early reading success.

Writing by Hand Improves Memory

Have you ever remembered something better because you wrote it down? That's not just your imagination—it's backed by science. Writing by hand forces us to slow down and think more deeply, which helps the brain store and retrieve information more effectively.

It Strengthens Fine Motor Skills

Every time a child holds a pencil, they're building muscles in their fingers, hands, and wrists. These fine motor skills are essential for everyday tasks like buttoning shirts, tying shoelaces, using scissors, and opening lunch containers.

Encourages Focus and Self-Control

Handwriting helps kids develop executive function skills like attention, working memory, and self-regulation. When children write by hand, they have to focus, stay on task, and hold an idea in their mind while moving their hand to produce it.

Supports Creativity and Confidence

There's something magical about seeing your own thoughts take shape on paper. Whether it's writing a name, a story, or a single letter, handwriting helps kids express themselves and feel proud of their growing abilities. .

The Power of Art and Coloring for Growing Minds

Art and coloring aren't just fun—they're essential to how children grow, learn, and make sense of the world. From boosting creativity to supporting emotional well-being and brain development, drawing and coloring provide a foundation for many skills kids will use for a lifetime.

Boosts Brain Development

Engaging in drawing and coloring activates both hemispheres of the brain. The creative right side is stimulated by imagination and expression, while the logical left side helps with planning, spatial awareness, and fine motor coordination.

Strengthens Fine Motor Skills

Like handwriting, coloring within lines, holding crayons or pencils, and making intentional strokes all help develop the small muscles in the hands and fingers.

Encourages Self-Expression and Emotional Processing

Art gives children a safe space to express emotions they may not yet have words for. Through art, they can communicate joy, frustration, curiosity, or fear.

Supports Focus, Relaxation, and Mindfulness

Coloring has a calming effect on the nervous system. The repetitive, structured nature of the activity helps children relax, focus, and practice mindfulness.

Fosters Imagination and Creative Thinking

Art encourages kids to explore, make choices, and take creative risks. These early experiences lay the foundation for problem-solving, innovation, and flexible thinking.

If children are inspired to write more, you can duplicate the next page to make matching lined writing paper!

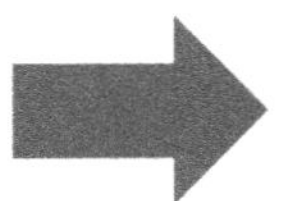

Your feedback is greatly appreciated!

It's through your feedback, support and reviews that we're able to create the best books possible and serve more people.

We would be extremely grateful if you would take a few minutes to leave an honest review of the book for others to see.

To do so, simply find the book on Amazon's website (or wherever you purchased it) and locate the review section. On Amazon, look for the star ratings at the top of the listing and click the number to the right. That will take you to the ratings where you'll see the option to "Review this product" as shown below. Select a star rating and write a sentence or two. That's it!

Thank you so much for your support!

Check out our other
Color & Write books--including
*Color & Write:
Animals of North America*

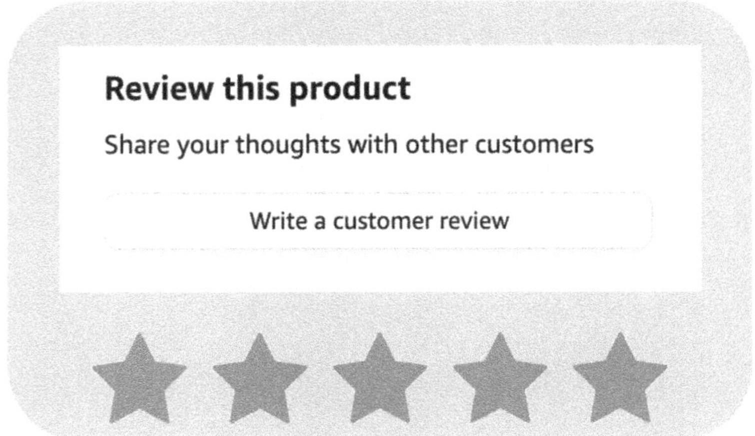

www.ingramcontent.com/pod-product-compliance
Lightning Source LLC
Chambersburg PA
CBHW041033050726
47599CB00018B/1951